"Part documentary, part soap opera, this MTV series takes a peek at the lives, loves and petty disputes of a group of twenty-somethings . . . a real set of roommates—an unlikely concept in a TV universe filled with trumped-up and pumped-up reality."
 —Rick Sherwood, *The Hollywood Reporter's* Salute to
 The Real World on its 100th episode

"The program attracts more than 40,000 applications per year; it's easier to get into Yale." "*The Real World* is an insult to anyone who lives in the real world."
 —*People*

"These are real people who, despite their best efforts to act cool for the cameras, drop their facades from time to time and reveal their true emotions, dreams, fears and prejudices."
 —David Bianculli, *Daily News*

"What happens to these folks happens in the real world: distractions, conflicts, divergent goals. Pretty soon, the business ends up being beside the point."
 —Christopher Caggiano, *Inc.*

"How long can MTV milk this formula?"
 —Ken Tucker, *Entertainment Weekly*

"[You] can't erase the emotional scars left by allowing your volatile relationship to be presented to a national television audience."
 —*Total TV*

"The show's producers seem comfortable that what they bill as a reality-based soap opera is first and foremost entertainment."
 —Evan Perez, Associated Press

Livin' in JOE'S WORLD

Unauthorized,

Uncut,

and Unreal

The Memoirs of
JOE PATANE

from the Miami Cast of MTV's
The Real World

HarperPerennial
A Division of HarperCollinsPublishers

You can contact the author at the following addresses:
http: //members.aol.com/aaprjp/
HCJRP@aol.com
P.O. Box 8465, New York, NY 10116

All photographs © Joe Patane or the photographer if known.

HarperCollins books may be purchased for educational, business, or sales promotional use. For information please write: Special Markets Department, HarperCollins Publishers, Inc., 10 East 53rd Street, New York, NY 10022.

FIRST EDITION

Designed by Elliott Beard

Library of Congress Cataloging-in-Publication Data

Patane, Joe.
    Livin' in Joe's world : unauthorized, uncut, and unreal / Joe
  Patane. — 1st ed.
      p.   cm.
    ISBN 0-06-095277-6
    1. Real world (Television program : United States)   I. Title
  PN1992.77.R43P38 1998
  791.45'72—dc21   98-3578

98 99 00 01 02 ❖/RRD 10 9 8 7 6 5 4 3 2 1

Note from the Author

The following pages describe real events and real people to the best of my ability. If any errors of memory or judgment have crept in, I apologize for them.

To Nic, for bringing me to my knees
To God (not Dominic) for lifting me up

Contents

Contents

Acknowledgments

Coming to an understanding of what is really real after this experience was quite a challenge for me and involved many people to bring it all together and make sense of it. Thank you to all those who jogged my memories, both good and bad. Writing it all down and gathering it into this book was the best thing I could think of to reach my own new reality. I wish all the cast members and everyone who has been affected by the show could do the same. The words "thank you" are underrated these days, and kind words are hard to come by in the big city. Everybody's "too busy" to share them with each other. But I want to thank *all* the members of my family for what they've shared with me. They are who I am.

To all *Real World* cast members, past, present, and future, their families, friends, lost loves, and everyone around them who were and may continue to be negatively impacted by the show: believe in yourselves and your loved ones, communicate (patiently), and live again.

Acknowledgments

To Father O'Hare and the entire Fordham University community, especially Residential Life: The Fordham experience has expanded my mind, and the Jesuit emphasis on getting to know and understand the whole person was and still is very real for me. I am proud to be part of this vital academic institution.

To Tracy James, Young Tiger Productions, and Andre LaPlume.

To Fathers Mullin, Grimes, Ned, Piderit, Reedy, O'Malley, Hentges, and Pierce, and Sisters Steeley and Deiters.

To Sue Dean, Pat Farabaugh, Mike Hayes, Joonmo Ku, Thomas Gentile, and Rich Ponticello.

To Dad for talking to me. To Mom for listening. And again, to my entire family, for still loving me.

To Drs. Sheila, Amelio, Sarah, Susan, and Sharon, and psychology professionals everywhere for helping people like me out of the funk.

To Mr. Verde, Mr. Mucciolo, Mr. McQuillan, and teachers and parents everywhere: through all the frustration, you do reach some students and it is worth it to us whether we show our appreciation or not.

To Perry Verrino, Andy McCruden, Carmen Cabalero-Ramos, Arlene Eager, Steve DiSalvo, Matt Brown, Virginia Fenton, Skip Doyle, Alicia Inafuku, Steve Wozniak, Kersten Larson, Bruno Santonocito, Bert Twaalfhoven, Sue Watkins, Joan Sain, Ron Bajakian, Bruce Prevo, Sharon Smith, Ernest Scalberg, Jim Stoner, Frank Werner, Lauren Mounty, Margery Covello, Jaak Jurison, Mike Marenick, George Blake, and everyone else who gave a little guy with a lot of energy the tools and responsibility to race ahead.

To you for reading this book from cover to cover and reflecting on your own self-awareness and improvement. No answer is

Acknowledgments

ever outside of your life unless it is a reflection of you. The reality is inside us. (Public access cable guy 11/18/97).

To Lee Miller, Kevin McShane, Mauro DiPreta, Liana Fredley, Kevin Powell, and Brian Monaco.

To those who rejected me in my business and personal life. You made me strive for bigger and better things. A family member once wrote to me: "Make an energetic effort to seek the goodness and talent and successes of those around you. The journey to your own self-worth is in confirming with others their own. Your family will always love you." I certainly love them.

To Cordell Brown, Dan Devine, Paul Daly, George Tan, Nes, Serg, and many others who I have hurt for not being in touch and more.

To everyone at St. Ignatius Summer Camp in Crown Heights, Brooklyn. To the St. Paul the Apostle, St. Francis Xavier, and Sisters of St. Ursula communities. To the Career Awareness Program students, and administrators at the Fresh Air Fund in New York City. To Cousin Kris and the extended Woz family, Dan Magner, and Bobby, the blind "Mayor of 23rd Street": you all made me see again.

And to everyone who has touched my life. Not being mentioned here does not mean you mean any less to me.

In memory of my Godparents, Dorothy Ianora and Anthony Reitano, and also David Connors.

Powered by, and thought differently with, Apple Macintosh.

Introduction

I write this book for closure. Closure to a part of my life that I had difficulty facing and accepting, part of my life I didn't understand or want to admit to, part of my life that's over and I can now move on from. I really recommend to everyone to take the time—a whole lot of time, if necessary—to get to know and love the most important person in your life: yourself. Then, and only then, can you truly love another.

My life is not a television product. I'm still plain old Joe. I went through all this and I learned and changed, but I haven't been beaten by the show, like many others appear to have been. MTV and Bunim-Murray productions were not involved in the production of this book at all. Even so, the goal of *Livin' in Joe's World* is not to bash or blame them for everything that has (or hasn't) happened in my life over the past years. It's more about getting down to what's real and what's not real. I definitely lost my sense of reality being involved in this show. Until I had cameras surrounding me twenty-four hours a day, seven days a week, for five and a half months, and lived with a microphone constantly attached to my waistband, I was truly unaware how much I cherished my privacy. I didn't even know what was private in my life until I went through something like this.

My plan here is to present a clear, fair, realistic picture of what happens when you allow yourself to be placed in the public eye, without preparation for how it will affect the rest of your life. For better or for worse, a portion of my life is recorded in history. And like so many other events in history, it wasn't always recorded accurately. This is my chance to share my version. This is a chance to tell my story, the more true story, without being censored or creatively edited. I honestly feel that the show exploits young people without taking into account the ramifications and psychological impact the show has, not only on cast members and others who appear on screen, but on almost everyone close to them.

The following pages attempt to take readers to the level I had hoped to take viewers to when I agreed to be on the show, where they understand how much all people have in common and how much potential we have to do what's right. I go beyond the series to explain the off-camera drama, bumbling business dynamics, psychological breakdowns, mega–power trips, creative editing, manipulative and invasive camera tactics, and emotional turmoil generated by the show. I do hope you enjoy it.

Livin' in
JOE'S WORLD

CHAPTER ONE

What Possessed Me?

This is the true story of seven strangers picked to live in a house (have their lives taped) and start a business, to find out what happens when people stop being polite and start getting real.
—MTV's The Real World, *Miami series, opening statement*

Hi, I'm Joe, former cast member of MTV's *The Real World,* and believe it or not, I made it out alive. I had no idea what I was getting myself into when I was selected to be on the show. It boiled down to five and a half months of extreme insanity. Everything from my personal life to my spiritual life drastically changed. I had zero privacy. Even when I went to the bathroom, a camera tried to follow me. I don't know if you can imagine this sort of experience, but it's certainly not common in any other *real* world. Considering the living conditions, I find it amazing that I actually *did* make it out alive. After spending a couple of years recuperating from living in MTV's *Real World,* I'm finally ready to talk. And believe me, there's plenty to say about how *unreal* MTV's *Real World* really is!

How I Got Hit by the Real World

It all started when I was surfing the Internet and found myself in the MTV on-line area, where I saw that MTV was casting its fifth season of *The Real World* in Miami Beach. I figured, What the heck, why not go for it! Especially because MTV was adding a new slant to this particular season: they planned to give the cast $50,000 in start-up capital to begin their own business. *Ca-ching!* They were talking my language. With business-school expenses and bills mounting, I was looking for an opportunity to take on new personal, professional, and potentially financially rewarding challenges. My longtime buddy Mike Hayes could tell that I was intrigued by the business aspect, and he encouraged me: "Joe, go for it! What have you got to lose?"

Mike and I had spent lots of time together at Fordham University channel surfing, and occasionally we'd run across the Los Angeles installment of *The Real World.* We weren't addicted to the show, but if it was on, we'd watch. Sometimes we joked about what it would be like to be on the show. I remember watching those episodes thinking, Man, this is so silly looking. There's so much more I could bring to the show. I always imagined it would be a good experience, an opportunity to share my unique perspective with the world.

Apply Pressure

When I applied to be on *The Real World,* MTV requested a five-to-ten-minute video that captured me "just doing my thing," explaining why I wanted to be on the show. I figured the best way to do that was to show them around my three-bedroom apartment in Manhattan. I talked my buddy Nestor into filming my audition video for me.

At the time, I was two classes away from finishing my strategic-management and international-business concentrations for my master's degree, and I had a job as resident director of a brand-new twenty-story residence hall housing about seven or eight hundred students at Fordham University, located in midtown Manhattan. It was a really cool place to live and work, and it was only a minute's commute to classes and my office. Fordham paid my salary by picking up the tab for my room, board, and tuition and giving me a living allowance besides. Not a bad deal, huh?

As Nestor rolled film, I showed off my "wall art"—my view of the Hudson River—and generally gave the grand tour of the apartment. I'd converted one bedroom into an office, which was where I made my livelihood running a small computer-consulting company called Computane Corporation. Deep down, I'm a big technology-business nerd, which is a trait I thought would work to my advantage during *The Real World*'s selection process. To my knowledge they'd never selected a person with heavy computer background to be on the show, and I knew that if they planned on starting a business, they'd better have somebody who knew how to use one.

Under my computer-nerd exterior lies the heart of a great big kid. When I applied to be on the show, I was twenty-five going on ten. I made sure to point this out in the audition tape by showing off my G-rated movie collection—*Aladdin, The Lion King, The Little Mermaid*—and the poster of a high school play I had been in that mirrored my life, *How to Succeed in Business Without Really Trying.* I also shared my family of stuffed animals, collected from the time I was born, including my first stuffed Snoopy. (My favorite character in the world is Snoopy. Just check out the *Real World* 1997 calendar and you'll see. United Media sent me lots of Snoopy goodies to parade around the house and during photo shoots for the press. I own tons of Snoopy paraphernalia—clocks, sheets, calendars, mugs, you name it.)

As a resident director with a team of awesome residence lifers, I had a staff of resident assistants to help take care of the building, the facilities, counseling issues, roommate conflicts, first aid, and emergency situations—anything that involved the well-being of the residents in the building. I loved it! I loved the diversity of the staff and students and loved being able to deal with their different personalities. It was a great mix of people, and I learned something from each and every one of them. It seemed to make sense that if I could live with so many students with such diverse backgrounds from all over the world under one roof, I could get along with six new strangers on *The Real World*.

At the end of the video I said, "I think being on *The Real World* would buy me time to decide whether or not running my own business is the thing for me. So give me a chance. I'd love to do it. I'm sure I'd bring a lot to the show. So thank you very much. Joe Patane, New York City, here I am, waiting for your call. Hope to see you soon. Bye-bye."

The Questionnaire

I sent in the videotape just in time to make their deadline, and waited for a response. A few weeks later, I received a massive twelve-page application, full of highly personal questions. This was MTV's way of getting to know everything about the applicants. Before I had a chance to become intimidated by its size and intrusiveness, I recruited two buddies, Mike and Serge, to help me answer the questions.

We put it together in less than a day. One part asked how other people would describe me. Mike answered, "Joe is outgoing, confident, and a babe magnet. He's also cocky, condescending, and impatient." He wasn't kidding. I'm the first to admit that I could be a cocky jerk at times. Luckily, I've come a long way in the past couple of years, enough that my friends have noticed the change and, more important, respected me for it.

Little did I know that the questionnaire would be the beginning of a long getting-to-know-myself process. I have to admit, if I filled out the same questionnaire today, I'd answer many questions differently. Some of the answers are embarrassing to read now, especially on issues of dating and women, because my outlook has changed so dramatically over the past couple of years.

For instance, at the time I applied, I believed in sex on the first date, reasoning that this immediately got the sexual tension out of the way and left room for a more open and honest relationship to grow (or not). This belief and some severe control-related issues caused many problems in my relationships. I used to make girls cry for fun. I enjoyed emotionally messing them up. I hurt several women this way. Then I started dating Nic, and all of my perceptions changed. She brought me to my knees.

Somehow I managed to spit out all this personal information into their questionnaire, FedEx it back to Bunim-Murray Productions, and again, find myself waiting for their call. I must have said something right on the questionnaire, because a couple of weeks later, I was conducting my first phone interview with the *Real World* casting people.

They had asked me to videotape myself during the conversation and to mail them the video. I was so worried that I'd forget everything I wanted to say that I'd written myself a note listing key things I thought would spark their interest and get my foot in the door. It obviously worked.

The Drill

I felt an adrenaline rush of nervousness and excitement when I went in for my first casting interview at MTV's New York City office location. I had to wait for some time while others were being interviewed, but the casting assistants took care of me. They were organized like clockwork. They even boosted my confidence by saying how psyched they were that I had made it this far and that they were pushing for me. It seemed odd that people knew me so well already when I didn't know them at all. That was just a taste of what was to come.

I settled into a room with several people and a camera sitting on top of a tripod, aimed at my chair. Despite the camera, I felt relatively comfortable. The interviewers were extremely friendly and made me feel welcome and relaxed. We exchanged a few niceties, then launched into an interview.

Straight out, the interviewer asked, "So, Joe, when was the last time you had sex? In the last six months, who have you been with and how many times?" I'm thinking, did my priest hire you to find out what I haven't been admitting in confessional, or what?

If they didn't get what they wanted to hear, they'd push a little further, pry a little deeper. This was another taste of what was to come. Being drilled with questions made me think things through, and challenged me to figure out how I really felt about hard-core issues. No one had ever challenged me so emotionally before. They'd perform a total interrogation, just short of water torture. I gave them all the information they asked for, knowing that this would be the only way to survive the process and leave the pack of thousands in the dust.

"Okay, Joe, tell us what your career goals are." Good, I thought, that's an easy one. "My ultimate career goal is to become the chairman and CEO of a *major* corporation someday, maybe my own, when it grows. I started my own business, Computane Corporation computer consulting, when I was twenty. I was getting paid for my computer knowledge at an early age and decided to learn how a corporation really works by starting one. So I got a lawyer, an accountant, and the rest is history. I'd like to expand someday."

They wanted to know what I'd bring to the group to help start a business. "The fact that I've done it before," I answered. "I'm a Brooklyn boy at heart and have plenty of street smarts and negotiating tactics."

I became more comfortable in the chair, and described how I'd gotten a taste of working on Wall Street. It began as an after-school job for J. P. Morgan that turned into a full-time position when I graduated from Fordham's Undergraduate College of Business in the Bronx. I worked as a business-systems analyst, which is basically the guy who makes technology less intimidating to people. I bridged the gap between the two worlds because I speak both languages.

I knew from the outset I wouldn't last very long on Wall Street. J. P. Morgan was a formal, bureaucratic environment—definitely not my style. On top of that, my manager underestimated my potential and seemed to limit my growth within the technical field. She understood technology but seemed to have limited skill for managing people.

"In addition to my bad work situation," I continued, "I was in a frustrating relationship. My girlfriend at the time, and her parents, couldn't comprehend or accept my entrepreneurial spirit and desire to take calculated risks. When J. P. Morgan offered me a comfortable job in Delaware that provided stability, steady income, and health benefits, it represented everything they craved and seemed to expect from me. To resign meant turning down their relocation package and relying on my personal business to support me. It also meant letting go of the girl I'd loved for over five years. Big decisions, but the right decisions.

"So I took off, went back to Fordham, enrolled in grad school at the Lincoln Center campus, and became a resident director. . . . I put in another two and a half intense years working and studying before applying to be on *The Real World*."

The interviewers went on to cover all aspects of running a business: How would I feel about working with six strangers, what type of business would I propose starting, what was my attitude toward teamwork, and would I be committed to the business once it was up and running?

"What issue are you passionate about?" they asked, and I responded, "If there's any issue I'm passionate about, it would have to be education. I've worked hard for mine, and still want to continue learning. You can't put a price tag on the value of knowledge. I think everyone should have a shot at a good education, and be passionate about wanting to learn all they can. When our brain stops ticking, so do we."

Then the interviewer asked about my two years as a residential-hall assistant and two years also as a resident director at Fordham. As a residence lifer, I explained, I was dedicated to being there when anyone needed someone to talk to; I tried to help prepare them for the "real world." I also explained how Fordham encourages students to live in the residential halls because they offer greater opportunity to realize personal and business goals while learning individual responsibility.

The next question was "Do you believe in God?" I responded, "I'm a practicing Catholic, you know, Sunday Mass every week, holidays, that sort of thing. I perceive God as my buddy. He's always with me."

The casting people coaxed me to further discuss my belief in God. It wasn't enough to share my relationship with Him, they wanted me to talk about the burning of the cross. And they wouldn't stop there.

Eventually all questioning turned toward sex. "So, about your sex life . . . what exactly do you do on a daily basis? How promiscuous are you? Describe your current sexual activity. How often do you have sex? Alone or with a partner? Daily? How do feel about homosexuality? How would you feel about living with a homosexual who might be attracted to you?"

When they got around to drilling me about my family life, I began by describing my parents' relationship. "While I was growing up, my dad flew planes and wasn't around much. Whenever he was home for a few days, my parents would, lovingly, argue a lot. When my father retired, it was the worst. But now my parents have mellowed and I actually see them sneak a smooch here and there. I imagine my dad wants me to get married—he loves grand-children.

"My parents always handled conflicts diplomatically. I was the youngest of eight brothers and sisters in a small house in Brooklyn. The standard 'wash your dirty mouth out with soap' and 'be good or you'll get the belt' scare tactics seemed quite effective for all. To toughen me up, my brothers would push me around. They also pushed each other around. My sisters would pull hair. I fought a lot with my sisters. They screamed at my brothers and vice versa. It was one big happy family."

The interviewer leaned forward. "What are you afraid of?" I leaned back. "My greatest fear is wasted time. It really bothers me when I see people wasting their time and not realizing their potential. There's so much out there to grab hold of and love. I just want to live life, strive for love and happiness, and share it with the world."

Then they wanted to know, "If selected, is there any person or part of your life you'd prefer not to share?" I thought about it and answered, "Not at this point. Out of respect to my family members, I'd like to ask them to be specific about what I could and couldn't share about them. They don't know I'm applying to be on this show, but I think they'd be psyched if I made it."

Finally they asked, "Joe, do you have any bad habits we should know about?" I answered, "Well, I should probably mention that I'm pretty hyper and impatient. But the only habit I really have is a tendency to smile quite a lot."

Throughout the whole tedious interview process, I never thought I would actually get on *The Real World*. For me, being interviewed provided a way to learn more about myself. It became a fact-finding adventure, unraveling all kinds of surprises I never knew I had buried in there. I subjected myself to their questions because I was learning so much about myself. It was like getting personal counseling session after personal counseling session for free. I shared information I would never, *ever* share under any other circumstance. It was actually refreshing, because they listened intently and appeared interested in me. My good friend and life mentor, Sue Dean, once remarked, "Joe is very daring in search of the truth. That's one of his strongest qualities. I know people decades older than he, who would not dare look at themselves in the bold way that he's willing to do." This series of interviews certainly dared me to face my strengths and weaknesses head-on.

I went through something like eight callbacks. I did a lot of talking. The whole process is a blur.

Call Waiting . . .

Waiting for MTV's phone call gave me plenty of time to consider how I would feel if selected. I wasn't afraid of living with six complete strangers, mainly because I came from a big family. I wanted to put myself in a risky situation. I considered myself independent, but wanted to develop deeper self-awareness. Sue describes this desire as provoking all the lessons we want to learn. If we want a time of ease and comfort, we find a way to have that. If we want to stir things up so we can look at our lives from a new perspective, we provoke that. I was driven to explore—I was ready to stir things up!

During the interview process I came to some surprising revelations. For example, I learned just how seriously I took my relationship with Nic. This came as a pleasant, yet scary, surprise. Outwardly I acknowledged we shared something special, but the interviews made me confront and accept the depth of my love for her. I felt assured that this love would give me the strength and support to survive the challenges I would face on *The Real World*.

Based on my old way of thinking, the idea of living in a house with attractive women would have seemed like a temptation to cheat on Nic. But I knew this was no longer true. I knew I could handle the situation, with Nic's help. I figured, No problem, I totally love Nic, I want to be with her, I'll never cheat. It'll be a challenge, but I'm up for it. This was the first time I was able to talk openly about a woman in this way. My past is clouded with relationships I consider disrespectful to women, and this was a chance to redeem myself. I was going to Miami Beach to start a business, not to fool around.

I also tried to imagine starting a new business venture. I considered myself a suit-and-tie kind of guy when it came to business, and I assumed if I was chosen to be on the show, my roommates would share a similar work ethic. Everyone else being interviewed must be getting drilled with the same questions, I thought. Which meant the casting people were looking for six other people with similar answers and a passion for starting a business. This way, they could ensure the greatest chance for success right from the start. Now that the show's over, I'd love to see how everyone else answered those questions, because my theory certainly didn't hold true.

The interview process started in October, and by Christmas I began thinking this venture might become a reality. I needed support to continue divulging the intensely personal information the casting people were digging for, so I gathered my family and friends around the Christmas tree and let them in on my covert application process. I got an overwhelming endorsement from all: "You're crazy, but go for it!"

My mom remembers it differently: "Before Joe went on the show, he asked the family if anyone objected. Of course, no one knew what it would entail at that point—we told him that it was his business. All we asked was that he earn his final six credits and earn his degree, which would be no easy task being on *The Real World*."

I was particularly sensitive to how my Sicilian father would react to my involvement in the show. He comes from a world completely different from mine. He was eighteen months old when my grandparents brought him and his five-year-old sister over on a boat to the United States from Italy. His sister died from scarlet fever on the way. My dad is the best, he just comes from a different generation, and we have different definitions and understandings of the worlds we live in.

I promised my parents that I would finish my MBA while I was in Florida. I knew they would support my decision to be on the show if I was able to keep this promise. My girlfriend, Nic, *supposedly* supported me as well. Later I would learn that she wanted to use my absence as a way to push away from our relationship. Little did any of us know what we were in for.

Before the casting people made their final decision, they sent a camera crew to follow me around. Talk about building up the suspense! The cameramen tagged along as I did the rounds at Fordham and chilled out in my apartment, trailed behind Nic and me on the streets of Manhattan, and more. I got a little flavor of what it would be like to live in front of the lens for five and a half months. It was exciting because I got treated like a celebrity in my own little ordinary world.

People kept asking what was going on, and why a camera was following me, but I couldn't say. I was instructed not to reveal the identity of the crew and show. "We're filming a documentary," they'd say, if anything at all. Everything had to be kept as confidential as possible.

Caller ID

Many months, written pages, personal and phone interviews later, *Ta-dah!* I got the phone call that went something like, "You've been chosen to be on *The Real World*! Drop everything! Pack your bags and come on down! You've got one week! And by the way, don't tell anyone about this. We'll take care of the media-hype thing later! *Trust us!*"

I was rushed to sign a big fat contract on the last day of interviews, and certain casting people told me not to make any changes. They made it clear that thousands and thousands of people wanted to be on the show. I didn't have time to read between the lines because of the pressure to sign, and I had no bargaining power anyway. For better or for worse, I signed a twenty-five-page contract to be on *The Real World* for five and a half months. I suppose it was just an oversight that their bulky contract neglected to mention the therapy that many of us would need when the show wrapped.

> We let them know, Look, basically you'll be doing this just for the experience. You don't get residual checks, this isn't going to open up the doors of Hollywood for you. What you'll be getting is the experience and enough money to buy a midsize used car.
>
> —*coproducer Jonathan Murray, Bunim-Murray Productions*

Sarah, one of my fellow cast members, once said, "I think Joe got picked because one of the chicks liked his voice—that's what I heard. She was so enamored by his accent. . . . And also . . . she said he'd be, like, a king-pin for getting the business going." The main reason I went for the show—and I *thought* it was why we were all picked—was to make a difference. I wanted to prove that young people have the know-how and energy to run a business, that we have a voice and can create something decent with all of our energy. I've had my own computer-consulting business since I was twenty, and became an expert in the field of outsourcing information technology. Because of this and other professional experience, I'm really into promoting the importance of having an education, doing internships, and traveling. I don't drink or smoke, I'm highly energetic, and I thought I would be a positive role model for people of the so-called MTV generation. I wanted to use the show as a means to get my word out. I would soon discover this was a grand naive plan indeed!

CHAPTER TWO

The First Signs

As soon as I met Flora, I knew I was finished.
—*a frightened me*

Welcome to Miami

I had six days to pack and prepare for the big move to Miami. The only thing I knew was that they had sent me a plane ticket and one of my new roommates would be joining me on the flight from New York City to Florida. The producers made sure a film crew was set up in my apartment when the roommate, Flora, phoned to make arrangements.

Nic wanted to support me but didn't want to be around when Flora showed up. She hates good-byes to begin with, and really hated the fact that I was flying to Florida with a woman. So my buddy Mike came with me in the van to the airport to see me off. Together we were introduced to Flora for the first time. He agreed, I was doomed!

Flora's sunglass-clad attitude early in the morning was enough to darken the brightest of days. I had never met this woman, she had just arrived from Boston, and here she was, presenting herself in a way that said, "Look, pal, this is who I am, I'm not all that interested in getting to know you, and if you don't like it, well, too bad. Stay on your side of the plane, and we'll get along just fine." The first thing she said to me when I saw her face-to-face in the van was, "You're late!" She had dark red sunglasses and a Walkman on and went on and on about how tired she was and how she was doing the show a favor by being on it. It was ridiculous. She seemed somewhat like a female version of Puck, the problem member of the San Francisco cast. I tried to be sociable, but she said she had a headache and didn't want to be disturbed. It wasn't being in front of the cameras that made me speechless for the first time in my life, it was Flora's attitude that did it.

A few weeks before leaving to be on the show, I had gotten some form of food poisoning. It must have happened when I tried using my Christmas-gift wok with Nic for the first time. Evidently, we didn't cook the chicken enough, or I didn't initially clean the wok enough, or something, because the next thing I knew, I was doubled over with stomach cramps for days. The hospital diagnosed it as, no surprise, "some form of food poisoning" and even removed an aggravated lymph node as a precaution. The procedure left a scar on my neck that you can clearly see in almost every episode. I wasn't sure if I was still feeling queasy from the operation, or just from meeting Flora for the first time.

After our introduction, Flora said on camera, "Joe smiles too much. I don't trust people who smile too much." Well, if I smile too much, she certainly frowns too much. For her to make a comment like that seemed a true sign of her inner hurt and pain: it seemed she couldn't deal with someone who was more happy than she was. I thought that despite her outward negativity toward me, perhaps deep, deep, deep, *deep* down, she had a good heart. I was *hoping* that, anyway.

I wasn't sure if I should even get on the plane after meeting Flora. If the rest of the group had the same self-important outlook, there wasn't much chance of ever getting a business off the ground. But it was obviously too late to back out.

Flora and I made small talk on the way from the airport to Miami. She didn't have much to share between Walkman songs, but she did let me carry her luggage. Believe me, that was headway. We arrived in Miami the night before the official "move-into-the-house day," so the show put us up in a Miami hotel by the dock where we'd take a SeaTaxi to the house the next morning. I have no idea what Flora did that night, but I spent it shacked up in my hotel room, quiet and alone, trying to get some sleep and recover from the day's chaos. I wanted to be energized when I met the other members of the house. I was already spent from meeting just one.

The next morning, we checked out of the hotel and boarded the SeaTaxi. I thought this was a nice way to make an entrance, zipping up to *The Real World* house from the bay. Even Flora showed signs of enthusiasm for the first twenty minutes of the boat ride. By the time an hour had passed, however, we wondered if we'd ever get there. Evidently, the SeaTaxi driver couldn't drop us off because the directors had orchestrated everyone's arrival and we were ahead of schedule. So the driver circled the bay for a couple of hours. Once the novelty of being at sea wore off, I fell asleep. When I awoke, we were docking at our destination, *The Real World* dream house. We knew which house was ours the minute it came into view—a hulking ultra-blue-and-yellow vision on Rivo Alto Island, a secluded residential area south of South Beach.

The House

While Flora scouted out the bedrooms to mark her territory, I aimed for the refrigerator and the pool table. The enormity of the house promised the consolation that I wouldn't have to spend every minute in the same room with Flora. I didn't realize then how claustrophobically small this place would seem over the course of five and a half months.

The fluorescent Ikea–meets–Dr. Seuss decor certainly jumped out at us under the bright studio lights. These lights, plus cameras, cables, and high-powered circuit boxes, filled every room of the house. None of the rooms had doors except for the bathrooms (and for some reason the showers had no curtains).

The house is at least two times bigger than what you see on television. Before we moved in, they completely gutted the house and divided it into two sections. We lived in one half and the other was used as office space and control rooms. We didn't get to see their half of the house until the wrap party on the last day we were there. Their wing housed the camera and film storage room, the crew's snack room, and other production facilities. The garage was turned into an electronics-packed surveillance room dominated by a wall of many monitors.

There were even certain areas on our side of the house that we were forbidden to enter because they housed video and/or sound equipment. The crew used hidden closets for the electronics, supplies, and control panels. The lights seemed to automatically turn on and off or dim at specific times during the day. The house functioned like clockwork. We knew when someone was going to come out of the little back room and turn everything on or take inventory of the cameras and equipment or replace a blown lightbulb. They kept careful tabs to make sure the motion-detector camera was detecting, the lights were in the right position, and the "props"—like our living-room furniture—were set perfectly. The crew routines were so regimented, it was almost like being in a jail. It wasn't until we were released that I made this comparison. Although I have never been to jail, I gotta imagine this is darn close.

The Gang's All Here

When the rest of the group started arriving, I thought, What a relief, they all look normal. Then I thought, Normal? What is *normal* anyway? When it came to sizing up my new roommates, I had to question my definition. I never knew such diversity until I entered that house in Miami Beach. I mean, I've lived around New York City all my life, but I never had the firsthand opportunity to experience the challenges of actually *living* so closely with individuals so unlike myself.

We quickly established that everyone in the cast was chosen to fit some kind of stereotype: Flora was the antagonistic Russian femme fatale, Cynthia was the down-to-earth African-American den mother, Melissa was the hot-tempered Cuban, Dan was the token gay guy, Mike was the all-American jock, Sarah was the skate-punk comic relief, and I was the business dude. Being a five-foot-six-inch guy with a six-foot fashion-model girlfriend also seemed to help create my "MTV image." I guess that makes good TV.

Right away, I tried to imagine running a business with my roommates. It seemed like an ideal situation—instant start-up capital, reliable investor, and free international television advertising. The show itself would be our greatest selling and marketing tool for any company we agreed to develop.

I figured our business had a chance at being successful because certain casting people gave me the impression they were selecting compatible business partners for the show. After we got the introductions out of the way, and went through the disaster of choosing bedrooms, we started sharing our enthusiasm and seriousness about how to get the business up and running. They exuded energy and eagerness to start as soon as possible, so I figured we were on our way.

A Day in the Life . . . The Regimen

A typical day in the house began with strapping on my waistband microphone immediately after my morning shower. The microphones were a big pain in the butt. They were bulky and they ran on batteries that had to be changed at least twice a day. Sometimes in the middle of important conversations, I'd find a sound person tapping me on the shoulder for a battery change. We couldn't wear the mike in the water, so sometimes jumping in the pool or the bay behind the house was a safe haven for a bit, until they broke out the Sony water-sports jam-cam. It was useless! Half the time we tried to forget they were on, and the other half we had to be conscientious about not damaging them. We had to make sure we didn't accidentally lose the clips that attached the actual mikes to our shirt or pull on the cables or the mike head, as this would destroy the mike. The units were incredibly delicate and everyone was paranoid about screwing one up, because we were constantly being verbally reprimanded about how expensive they were to replace and warned accordingly (though all those threats never amounted to anything).

When I was ready to go in the morning, I had to report my day's schedule to Billy, the coordinating producer. We had to call him every day with our schedule. This way they could assign a crew to follow each roommate for the day. They also armed us with pagers to carry everywhere and have turned on at all times, so they could get hold of us if we broke away for a minute. They even taped our mikes to the *on* position, so we wouldn't get any funny ideas. To talk to Billy, we used the "Bat Phone," located in a phone booth in the pantry (where all the free sponsor goodies like K2 Rollerblades, Kooshes, and board games were stored). As soon as we picked the phone line up, it dialed Billy wherever he was. That was the phone's sole purpose—it didn't even dial out.

Reporting every minor event to Billy became a bigger pain than living with protective parents who insist on knowing your every move. We had to inform him about our every waking moment, whether it was just a quick run to the store, grabbing a couple of burgers at McDonald's, golfing, or whatever.

With each camera crew that followed us came a "release guy." It was this guy's job to get people who got caught in the frame as they were filming us to sign waiver forms allowing them to appear "in any and all media throughout the world in perpetuity." If they refused to sign, at least in some instances that I saw, their faces got the scrambled-image effect when the show aired. He would pull people aside and hand 'em a release form that said something like, "Whoever signs this waiver understands that every moment spent with Joe is amenable—in any way, shape or form—to be video-taped, cut, edited, and marketed—in perpetuity, throughout the universe." In clearer language that basically meant Bunim-Murray productions and MTV would become richer. It wasn't Release Guy's job to encourage people to sign if they didn't want to, that was clearly considered the cast members' job. Sometimes I'd be in the middle of lunch and be asked to talk a skeptical waitress or friend into signing a release so they could use the "potential useful footage." I frequently thought to myself, How real is this? During my preliminary interviews, I don't recall the casting people asking if I felt comfortable getting complete strangers to sign waiver forms.

Before I left for Florida, I received a "Cast Welcome Pack" from the producers. It briefed me on what to expect and what was expected of me during the five and a half months. The packet included a supply of guest performer releases and I was encouraged to have them signed in advance by the people I was in regular contact with (e.g., family members, friends, and my girlfriend). They wanted me to send as many completed releases as possible to them before I arrived. Few of my friends and none of my family were willing to sign at the time. They weren't trying to be unsupportive, they just wanted to protect themselves from exploitation.

At first, we were all heavily aware of being on camera. I was self-conscious even while eating cereal, but it was especially bad when they hung over me like hawks for hours on end when I was working on my computer.

After a couple of weeks, we became really comfortable in front of the cameras. We'd forget they were there until we were halfway through picking our noses. This kind of stuff is all on film—and everybody did it—including the ladies. The girls got caught naked; the guys got caught naked; I'm sure some girls and guys even got caught naked together. There is a whole lot of stuff I would regret if I didn't believe I went through this whole process for a reason. We eventually slipped into our individual routines, becoming less self-conscious and more tolerant of the cameras.

The Commandments

The "Thou-Shalt-Not Commandments," as we called the list of rules in the Welcome Pack, laid down the laws of the house. We quickly learned that we'd kissed all forms of privacy good-bye when we signed the contract. That was reiterated to us frequently by the producers and directors of the show when we'd give them a hard time about it.

We were specifically instructed never to socialize with the crew. The focus of the show was our relationships with each other, not our relationship with the "invisible people." "Breaking the third wall" would destroy the illusion that the show was "real," we were told. We weren't allowed to say anything more than hello and good-bye for fear that the conversation would become more involved, which would alter the reality of the experience. I found this the most difficult rule to follow, especially in the beginning. It was clear (and actually verbalized by a couple of crew members) that we were seen as snotty, complaining brats. Politeness was a thing of the past now, as they tried to do their jobs and we tried to live our lives while keeping our end of the bargain. Closing doors on cameramen, not acknowledging their presence, took its toll on all parties and provoked feelings of animosity and tension.

They warned us not to mention MTV when referring to the experience. We could call it "the project," "a documentary", or come up with another expression. We couldn't tell people about MTV or *The Real World* while shooting. And for our privacy, we were only supposed to use first names while on camera.

We were forbidden to wear any type of clothing with a product logo when on camera. This meant rethinking my entire wardrobe. I never knew so much of my wardrobe sported brand names until I started packing. Sometimes the crew would just put masking tape over the logos so we wouldn't have to change. Even the Nike "swoosh" on my baseball cap had to be covered. We couldn't drink out of the cans or bottles because the logos would show, and all of the glasses in the kitchen were opaque so that the viewers couldn't see what we were drinking at all. I guess they only wanted to show logos if a company gave *The Real World* money or freebies to display their product. For instance, when we took flights in and out of Miami, regardless of the airline we traveled on, you'll only see one airline by name—and you'll see it over and over again.

We were required to spend every night in the house unless we were out of town. This rule even restricted those nights we'd want to spend in the hotels of friends or significant others when they came to visit. When Nic came to Miami, I had to be home by six or seven A.M. (before the night crew shifted with the day crew), wait for the day crew to report to them the coming events of my day, and either go back to my bed in the house, or go back to Nic's hotel room. I didn't have a car in Florida, so this became a big hassle and often a financial burden, since I was renting cars all the time just to have a slight feeling of freedom (even though the crew would be right in the backseat, or in a van driving right alongside me with the sliding door open and cameras rolling).

Everywhere we went had to be accessible to the crew, even when the door was shut. Many times, Nic and I tried to shut the crew out of her hotel room, and although they weren't physically in the room for brief periods of time, they must have used highly sensitive microphones to pick up almost every sound through the door.

We were responsible for the house and its contents. Should anything be unreasonably damaged (carpeting, light fixtures, appliances, etc.), the replacement cost would be deducted from our final payment. If we wanted to have a number of guests at the house, we had to get permission from the producers well in advance. That's one reason why you never see any crazy parties at the house. Luckily, I got out of there without owing them a cent. Sarah, on the other hand, had several friends who enjoyed raising a ruckus once in a while, and I'm sure she got reprimanded or maybe even docked for it, but she certainly didn't care.

There was a strict no-drugs-on-the-premises rule (including any area in the near vicinity of the house). This was vitally important, and enforced. Being a nondrinker, nonsmoker, and non–drug user, this was the easiest rule for me to follow. I can't say the same for *all* the others, however.

While they were shooting, all background noise had to be turned off. So of course that limited our freedom to watch television and listen to music. You'll never see us playing the stereo loudly because they couldn't edit conversational footage effectively if there was noise in the background.

We were *allowed to have a few friends visit at a time, but we had to be considerate of the other roommates.* Some roommates were more considerate than others, however. For example, when Mitchell, Flora's boyfriend from Boston, came to visit for an indefinite amount of time, many thought he would become our unwelcome eighth roommate. Luckily, I was out of town for that falling out among the roomies (Dan and Flora in particular).

I had several friends visit who never made it on camera, probably because they all seemed to get along with my roomies, and that certainly didn't make for good television. To this day, I believe that my buddies Tom and Andy didn't make it on-camera because they found out they were both attorneys. Most of the time, I had friends stay in hotels. This way, they had a little extra privacy and I had a place to escape from the confines of the house. Our friends weren't allowed to videotape or take photos of the crew while they were rolling. We could take photos or video-tape at other times, but photographing the video crew was off lim-its, because it distracted them or ruined potential footage, I guess.

We had to be discreet with the house address and phone number. Without even knowing it, we would be followed home or watched

The Confessional

Every week, we had to visit the Confessional, a pri-vate, soundproof room with a camera we operated ourselves, available twenty-four hours a day. Each week we were required to spend a minimum of fif-teen minutes in the video booth recording our thoughts, experiences, concerns, and problems—pretty much just talking to ourselves. Our tape was turned in one day prior to our scheduled weekly interview "on location" with the director. The Confessional was supposed to be used as our place to express our feelings about whatever we wanted to talk about. For me, it was the thing I always forgot to do before leaving on a trip back to New York, and I was constantly rushing through my weekly confes-sions right before my flights left out of Miami.

from the front of our house, or from the back bay. We were the talk of the town and it seemed like everyone wanted a piece of the action. Curiosity seekers would come up to the house, by land or sea, screaming, "Hey, this is the *Real World* house! Can we look inside?" We were right on the bay and people would cruise by in their boats, blowing their bullhorns, docking and walking onto our pool and patio area, trying to sneak a peek. Not even the high security and monitoring system installed throughout the house was enough to keep these people away. Oddly enough, a couple of our promotional bicycles and even a crew boat vanished. It was really . . . unreal.

Touching lights or equipment in the house was strictly off limits. They warned that everything was on or not on for a reason. If a crew member had forgotten to turn off the lights, we had to use the "bat phone" to have someone come turn them off. We found out how difficult it was to sleep with bright fluorescent lights shining overhead.

Every phone call that came in and every phone call that went out was recorded. Complete strangers sitting in the control room had access to any financial transactions we conducted over the phone, heard about family emergencies, recorded credit card numbers, and more. We were continually reminded to tell people they would be recorded during the call. I lost track of many family members and friends because I felt no one would want to have their phone conversations recorded. And just imagine what that kind of invasion does to a long-distance relationship! It's hard enough trying to maintain a geographically challenging relationship without having all that really deep, emotional stuff you say to your significant other—all the sexual innuendo, pet names, and sweet little baby talk—ending up on film and in some stranger's headset. That's intense—if a relationship isn't really strong, something like this is bound to destroy it, or draw two people closer a helluva lot faster. Nic and I experienced both effects at different times.

When we really wanted privacy on the phone, we'd run to a pay phone outside Walgreen's supermarket. Sarah and I went so often we were like a pay-phone tag team. We'd tell the crew we were going shopping, then beeline to Walgreen's. When they chose our house, they must have scouted for a place based on the distance from the nearest pay phone, because it was over a mile

Smile! You're on a Hidden Camera!

I'll never forget one of the most embarrassing realizations I made. At the end of taping, I was informed about the recording capabilities of a particular surveillance camera pointing at anyone speaking on the upstairs phone. For months I spoke on that phone thinking I had been allowed a little respectful, semi-private time to enjoy on the phone with Nic, without having an actual camera guy in my face. I knew they recorded every phone conversation, but I didn't know about the backroom surveillance monitors. I was speechless when this was revealed to me and I realized that an entire control room filled with people had seen me on the phone, when I assumed I was alone, touching myself, at times, where I shouldn't have been touching.

away. There were many times when we *tried* to sneak out of the house.

When I first got to Miami, these semi-private Walgreen's conversations preserved my relationship with Nic. We were doing well because we felt we could speak candidly, openly, honestly, and endlessly without the invasive cameras. In a couple of weeks, however, the crew finally figured out what we were doing. It turned out that the mikes also functioned as homing devices, so the crews always seemed to find us and could hear our end of the conversation anyway. Unfortunately, it took us a while to notice that. Watching the show, you can definitely tell when we aren't aware the cameras are filming us. The crew would hide in bushes, use telephoto lenses, and pick up our conversations with high-powered microphones. It really sucked to find that out later.

Aside from my hesitation to use the phones because they were tapped, I didn't contact many people from home when I first moved into the *Real World* house because I wanted to be strong and try to figure out how to handle my emotions and living situation without the help of others. I didn't think anyone could relate to my unusual experience. That was stupid.

Eventually, I started calling old friends more often. I realized the importance of this after making a major mistake with my good buddy Mike—I forgot his birthday. That was probably the warning sign to Mike that my life in Florida wasn't exactly ideal. Mike called me the day after his birthday and said, "Hey, how you doin', Joe? I'm just calling to see how things are going, and by the way, you kinda like forgot something . . . just letting you know." I couldn't figure out what the hell I'd forgotten until he told me. I felt like an idiot. That's when I finally admitted to him that I was having a hard time living in *The Real World*.

Three's a Crowd

The biggest confrontation between me and the camera crew occurred during intimate moments when I wanted to be alone with Nic. The crew got in the way and sometimes right up in our faces. They wanted controversy. They encouraged it! While I was trying to work things out with Nic, they were looking for the best camera angle.

In one of the episodes, you hear Nic and me talking, but only see the door of her hotel room. Nic had shut the camera crew outside. That's when she dropped a bomb—she told me she wanted to break up. She blocked out the cameras because she wanted to be discreet and allow me to deal with her bad news privately. That was cool of her and all, but little did we know the crew put a microphone up to the door or under the door so they could hear everything we were saying (even though we'd covered our personal mikes with pillows and sat on them), and much of it did make it on-air anyway.

The Getaways

The camera people hated it when we tried to outrun them. But there wasn't much they could do about it except bust our chops. They'd say, "You know Tom is going to be really upset about this." Most of us were afraid of Tom from the beginning. He was the director, and for some reason we never wanted to make him angry. Looking back, I'm not sure why I was afraid of Tom, except that he was the guy we had to answer to at the end of the week. It's not as if he would have thrown us off the show or anything, but he was generally the one who conducted the interviews and collected information on our plans. If we did something subversive to outrun the cameras, we had to listen to him complain about it. I guess that's what we all wanted to avoid, since he seemed to be the main guy who would be developing our personal "characters'" images. I remember crew members warning or joking (I didn't know the difference) that we should treat them right, or they'd make us look bad with things like unflattering camera angles.

As the Real World Burns

It was about week two when the honeymoon ended. One by one, we all blew up from the lack of privacy and inability to deal with our emotions. It was all fun and games until we started going insane. Flora put it well when she told a reporter, "You get into a fight with somebody and you go into your own room, and you just want to sit there pissed off—but there's always the camera watching you being pissed off." Melissa added, "Unless you are naked, the cameras are there." As Melissa and most of us found out the hard way, even when we were naked, if we were in a common open living area, even if a crew member was nowhere to be seen, somehow, someone or something was there to record it all—or just enough to make you and everyone close to you cringe in agony. At the beginning, I often just stayed in the house to chill and do my own thing while the others were out soaking up the Miami Beach scene. Even so, they always left a camera behind to film me, just working at the computer for hours. How boring it must have been for that poor camera person.

Extreme Close-Up

For me, watching *The Real World* on television is like looking in the mirror, except the image is more extreme—like a funhouse mirror. A mirror reflects a moment in time, it doesn't record your actions before or after that moment—good or bad. To see that reflection condensed, cut, and edited for television is quite a challenge for me and those close to me, who thought they knew me, but had their doubts. I even question who that person on television is at times, and it hurts. It's amazing that we lived in a house with a pool, a pool table, lots of toys, computers, every convenience, and none of us thought of the place as home. When I had the place to myself, it was okay, but it certainly wasn't home. Home is supposed to be a safe place.

CHAPTER THREE

The Roommates

Roommate Roster

Dan, 21: Student at Rutgers University, New Jersey, from
  Overland Park, Kansas

Melissa, 22: Cuban-American travel agent and phone-sex
  operator from Miami

Cynthia, 22: Waitress from Oakland, California

Flora, 24: Art-school student and bartender, emigrated from
  Russia to Brookline, Massachusetts, when she was three

Mike, 24: Restaurant manager and sports lover from Atlantic
  Beach, Florida

Sarah, 25: Comic-book editor and skateboarding free spirit from
  La Jolla, California

Joe, 25: Fordham University graduate business student from
  Brooklyn, New York

Scratching the Surfaces

"Burger anybody? Anybody want a burger? How about some veggies? No? Some chicken, then? Whadayasay. That's it. Nice. Everybody eat!" Nothing brought the roommates closer together or made us happier than the smell of food sizzlin' on the grill. I usually sprang for the spread because I loved to grill. For some reason, throwing raw meat onto an open fire and smacking it with a spatula provided some form of stress release for me. I grilled so often that my barbecues became legendary. I was big on chicken and turkey burgers, but always catered to the more red-blooded appetite with hamburgers, hot dogs, and the occasional kielbasa or London broil—mmmm. Mike would usually assist me, and ate anything. Cynthia went for the hamburgers because she thought she was too skinny and wanted to gain weight. Sarah, on the other hand, rarely sat down for a meal. Her idea of the perfect dinner consisted of Mike & Ikes, which probably explains her exceptional energy level.

Whenever I grilled, I always made enough for the roommates because I really did enjoy it. A couple of times I even ordered from Omaha Steaks and served up the quality stuff. I did hear the occasional "Thank you" from individuals in the group every once in a while, yet amazingly, I usually heard, "Joe, it's not cooked enough! Joe, this is burnt! You're making steak? But I don't eat meat." I appreciate honesty, but I prefer when it's delivered a bit more eloquently. The minute I started getting too many complaints was when I handed over the tongs and let my roomies do the flipping.

Eating seemed to be the only function we had in common.

The Lineup

Initially, the only assumptions we could make about each other were based on outward appearances, of course, but less obvious were the clues given by the contents of our luggage. The ladies had a variety of revealing personal possessions: Flora unpacked little more than cutoff shorts and halter tops, while Cynthia pinned her body-builder beefcake calendar to the wall. Melissa wheeled in the entire inventory of an upscale shoe boutique, and Sarah erected "Tchotchke City"—a crazy collection of bizarre toys that pervaded every available crevice in her parts of the house. On the guy side, Dan dumped nondescript dirty clothing into a bin and shoved it under his bed, Mike liberated his sunglasses and towel, and I booted up my computer.

We tried to play it cool in front of the cameras while we waited for everyone to arrive the first day, but we didn't know what the heck we were doing or how we were supposed to act. Under no circumstances did we want to come off looking like complete dorks, which is virtually impossible when you're extremely nervous. Obviously, we said and did things that make us cringe now, like when I was on that SeaTaxi ride to the house—I can remember I was so conscious of the cameras and my New York City ghost-white skin that I didn't want to remove my long-sleeved purple flannel shirt, no matter how hot it got on that first day.

I didn't start to relax until Sarah walked in, scoped out the house, declared, "This is dope!" and, fully clothed, dove into the swimming pool with me in tow. Talk about full-submersion baptisms. We were free at last from all the introductory tension and the wrath of Flora's stink eye. This act alone made Sarah and me kindred spirits for the rest of the season.

Unfortunately, our childlike abandon wasn't exactly embraced by the rest of the gang. Flora and Melissa started bitching at us for dripping water through the house and didn't stop bitching for five and a half months.

Neatness

The biggest surprise came when Sarah emerged as the neat freak in the group. She enjoyed cleaning up her messes almost as much as making them. It was never just a quickie, either. She made a project out of cleaning, unlike Dan. I don't recall Dan washing a dish, but he left plenty in the sink. The only time I remember Dan heavily cleaning was when his family came to visit. For him, tidying up meant wadding his unwashed laundry in with his clean clothing and shoving the ball under his bed.

Dan: Too Sexy for Miami

Once Dan landed a writing and subsequent modeling gig through the publisher of Miami's *Ocean Drive* magazine, he immersed himself in the role, spending long sessions gazing into the mirror, practicing his extensive range of expressions—the "Pout," the "Demure Sophisticate," the "Come-Hither Bad Boy," and the "Believe me, I'm a family man, oh, yes I am." The dude would be in the mirror for hours, playing with his face, creating different "looks." I understand that working in the mirror was part of his job, but he *really* got into it. He spent so much time staring into the bathroom mirror that he wouldn't even leave when we took showers. I don't know how he managed when the mirror steamed up.

I'm sure his photographer associates provoked this behavior, encouraging him to master his various looks, not the least of which was practicing looking straight. He was told by a photographer from his modeling agency something like, "You must be aware of your face, be aware of your features. You must develop sensitivity to the Rock Hudson syndrome." Which meant to me, "If you want to make it in this business, you can't look gay." That must've sucked for him to hear.

I'm sure it was difficult for Dan to compromise his longing to be completely out of the closet, and comfortable with his sexuality, in order to sustain his job modeling. But Dan learned early on that he could use his face and body to make a lot of cash. This wasn't his attitude when he arrived in Miami. When we first met, Dan was a real decent I'm-going-to-change-the-world-save-the-environment-hug-a-spotted-dolphin-fight-for-gay-rights student from Rutgers who wrote a popular column for his school newspaper. Miami transformed him into a guy who could make over a thousand dollars for less than a day's work standing around, making faces, posing, and putting on different cool clothes. He appeared to be losing his depth.

One of the perks Dan collected for working at *Ocean Drive* magazine and having a decent modeling portfolio (combined with having an MTV film crew attached to his hip) was dozens of invitations to happening events all over South Beach. Occasionally, he would "allow" his roommates to tag along. I give him credit for extending invites to us, because these were some of the only times everyone went out and did more upscale things together. Even if it was just a casual dinner, it was nice to be included. I wasn't much up for the more hyper stuff at that time, to the chagrin of my roomies.

Some of the roommates were definitely jealous of Dan's celebrity, feeling that Dan would get more screen time than the rest of us. My attitude was, "Go for it, Dan. You gotta strike while you're hot!" I was psyched when he invited us to his modeling events because I loved seeing him in action. It was funny: Dan was laughing all the way to the bank.

One night we all went for dinner and to a runway show at the Armani Exchange. It was the only formal fashion event I attended to see Dan in action. The minute I saw Dan come out from behind the curtain, dressed like a recruit from the Armani Army, I laughed and thought, Yeeeaah! Look at him! I mean, just *look* at him! This is great! He knew the minute he saw me in the crowd that he could relax and let go of his nervous jitters. That's the exact point in the show when he came back down to earth a bit and started having more grounded fun.

Dan felt really psyched when his parents and brother came to visit. Both he and his mom loved to ham it up for the camera—she even fought Dan for the mirror to make herself up. Whatever Dan lacked in the way of contributing to the food supply or cleaning of the house, his mom made up for by baking us severe Italian specialties and mounds of cookies. Feeding us was the quickest way to win our hearts and redeem Dan's soul. We liked her instantly and she even seemed to welcome Dan's boyfriend at the time, Arnie. During the show, she asked Dan why he didn't live with Arnie. She loved Arnie. We all did. I mean, hypothetically, I would want *my* son or daughter to move in with Arnie. But sometimes, when the person you're dating gets along too well with your parents, you don't want them anymore. Strange, but ever so true.

In my opinion, Dan's mother's approval was the kiss of death to Arnie. The minute Dan saw how well Arnie got along with his parents was the beginning of the end for Arnie and Dan. I'm sure there was more to it, but that's my take on the situation.

Dan had a truly cavalier attitude about dating, and it seemed he didn't really care who he hurt in the process. He figured, "I love Arnie and all, he's still in the picture, but it's okay for me to

Gender Questions

Dan had such a great time with his family that we had to cheer him up after they left. So Johnny, Mike, and I decided to take him to this restaurant in South Beach called Lucky Cheng's. We didn't exactly go for the food, although it is fine. We actually went for the ambiance and the wait staff, comprised of the most beautiful drag queens I've ever seen. It's nearly impossible to tell that they're guys, as Mike soon found out. We didn't want to spoil the surprise for Mike, so we didn't tell him about their gender secret.

As we stood outside waiting for a table, Mike was going nuts checking out these amazing-looking waitresses. Dan was friends with one of the wait-resses and arranged for "her" to give Mike lots of attention and really flirt with him. Mike had no clue that it was a man. He'll probably deny it to this day, but he thought this wait*er* was the hottest *wo*man in the world.

date other people, no big deal," without fully discussing this arrangement with Arnie or others. Dan also couldn't deal with the fact that Arnie was having trouble coming out to his own parents. That's about when Johnny came along. Johnny was cute and completely up-front and honest about his sexuality, and he fit right in to Dan's new Miami Beach modeling scene.

Dan, like many of us, was becoming a bit too confident and cocky with his bad self, which was a shame because he started out as a genuine, loving, dedicated, and committed person.

During their visit, Dan's dad quit coming to the house. He tried to face the cameras, but they got to him. I suppose he felt uncomfortable in front of them and couldn't overcome his uneasiness. He tried to do it for Dan, and once he actually said to me something like, "Joe, this is really difficult for me—I'm here and I'm talking to Dan, I'm trying to be supportive, but it's difficult." He didn't realize how hard it would be, and didn't want to create a scene. All I could do was listen and encourage him to communicate with Dan the way he could with me. It hurt Dan a lot. But his family made the effort to visit, and they tried to reach out—they really did try.

Mike: Real World Action Figure

It turned out Mike had also dabbled in modeling before coming to Florida, and he eagerly showed his portfolio to Dan in hopes of landing his own place within the fashion arena. Mike noticed Dan receiving much camera time and mad money doing the modeling thing and hoped to grab his own piece of the action. Instead, he landed an ad-sales job at the magazine, which turned Miami into a whole new land of opportunity for him.

Mike would come home from work about five times a day, hang out for an hour here or there, give or take, see if I wanted to join him for lunch, hit the beach, play golf, and chill on a daily basis—while he was "working." What a job! I'm sure he did his job as well as he had to. I'm just sayin' he seemed to have plenty of downtime. Not that I minded, because he certainly hooked me up with a few nice "working" lunches and other freebies around Miami.

Unquestionably, Mike had the business savvy, the managerial experience, and the number-crunching capability to enjoy this kind of leisure time and get paid for it. More importantly, he had what it took to *get away* with it. Mike got away with plenty of stuff in Florida, including what may be considered the most famous shower scene recorded in *Real World* history.

In regards to the Melissa, Mike, and Waitress shower scene, I heard at the [Boston] cast party . . . (this could be a huge rumor, mind you) that Melissa was, in fact, gay, and that Mike was used as a decoy so she could hook up with the . . . waitress—because Melissa didn't want that part of her life revealed on the show. Is this true?

—typical piece of fan mail

Not since Hitchcock's movie *Psycho* has a shower scene gotten so much attention. Ironically, *psycho* is a fitting description of the people involved in the shower that night. Let me just begin by saying that I can't believe this one incident became the highlight of the whole season—or at least the big unanswered mystery of the show. You can read what Mike and Melissa have to say in MTV's book, but all you really have to do, is closely watch the episode to piece together the puzzle. Another clue is when Sarah gives away specific details during the episode where Melissa leaves the house for good.

Either way, the following is my take on it all, without extra exaggeration or sound clips to distract you from whatever the truth may really be. The final call is yours.

It was one of those rare occasions when a bunch of the housemates got together to enjoy each other's company over some non–Joe-barbecued food and conversation. At the recommendation of Mike's *Ocean Drive* connections, and probably at their expense as well, we attended a local comedy club where Mike immediately hit it off with our waitress, Melody. She was eager to see our house and agreed to meet Mike when her work shift ended.

I was at home and in bed, trying to get some sleep, by the time Mike and Melody arrived at the house. I awoke to a few giggles and a big splash as Melody, Melissa, and a butt-naked Mike cannonballed off the dock and into the bay. I saw it just like the viewers would. They splashed around for a while, eventually deciding to take the party to the hot tub, I guess. This is where the craziness really kicked in. Their private grope session was captured by the undercover lens of an MTV surveillance camera and can be seen within the episode, if you observe carefully. Watching this closely should satisfy most curiosity seekers. No one can deny what's going on, as Mike and Melissa *both* seem to be enjoying Melody's company.

I was still trying to sleep when Mike came barreling in, begging me to create a diversion so the cameras wouldn't follow the threesome into the bathroom—the bathroom being the only safe haven where the cameras wouldn't journey if the door was closed. Since it was four or five in the morning, there weren't many crew members on duty, which worked to Mike's advantage. It was easier to outmaneuver one cameraperson as opposed to a whole fleet of cameras eager to get the all-important libidinous footage.

The crew knew they were outnumbered. They lived for moments like this, when a roommate hinted at the possibility of sexual behavior, and here they were with two roommates showing signs of just that. I guess the pressure was strong for the crew to get as much deviant activity on film as they could without actually spoiling the moments. So, needless to say, they weren't letting Mike or Melissa out of their sight. That's when I thought, what the heck, I can't sleep anyway, I might as well aid a roomie in need. So I bolted for the kitchen and tried to distract the cameras, since that's where Dan, Sarah, and Flora had already grouped to discuss the circus among themselves.

Mike's plea was heated, somewhat like, "You gotta help me out! The camera's up there! They're not giving me a break! Melissa's freaking about what the cameras might catch on film! Dude, help me out!"

They devised a covert plan to split up and meet in the bathroom, since one camera crew couldn't possibly follow all three people simultaneously. Melody was the first to run upstairs and lock herself in the bathroom. Then Melissa took the back route, and slipped in without being followed. When the camera crew finally figured out what was going on, we knew it would be tough to get Mike up and in there, but the boy was determined. Somehow he made it through the gauntlet without further assistance.

As the camera and sound guys tried to shove the boom microphone over and under the bathroom door, they triggered all the high-powered fluorescent stage lights in our bedroom, completely pissing me off. It was five in the morning or so by now, and there was no way I was going to get any sleep.

Meanwhile, Flora, Dan, and Sarah were hanging out downstairs, wondering what to do to make the most of the chaos. Looking for a better vantage point, they went outdoors and upstairs to listen outside the bathroom window. From there, they could at least hear the loud moaning and spanking noises that were coming from the bathroom. Never one to be left out, Flora decided to find out who was doing the moaning and who was doing the slapping.

With Sarah's assistance, Flora hoisted herself between the narrow slats of the window attempting to get a better view of the performance. Unfortunately, the combination of Flora's body weight and breast size caused the window to collapse, leaving her body hanging across the window pane, and alerting the bathroom trio to their presence. I'm sure they already knew someone was trying to watch through the window, but it didn't seem to matter, I guess. Mike may have been drunk past the point of action by that point, anyway, and Melissa had admitted to preferring voyeurism, so the soiree was ending anyway.

The group must have sworn Flora to secrecy, because whatever Flora saw, if anything, through that bathroom window, she never spoke a straight word about it. All I know is that Melissa was the one who drove Melody home, not Mike, and Mike wasn't the one doing the moaning.

Instead of going to sleep, Mike eventually flopped down on Sarah's bed to gloat about his exploits. I was relieved about this, since by that time, Sarah, Flora, Dan, and Cynthia had already convened in the boys' bedroom to get the lowdown, and the camera crew wouldn't turn out the lights and let me sleep until Mike had his eyes closed. It turned out Flora gave him a backrub and teased him about being a big stud. Then he tried to snuggle with Sarah. She squirmed for freedom, begging her stuffed bunny to help her get away from him. It seems they were just having fun and giving the camera some good closing footage. It was around six in the morning by then. The sun was coming up by the time everyone finally settled down.

Melissa Exposed

In the beginning, I rated Melissa as the most normal, decent, grounded person in the house. She had this conservative, good-Catholic-girl persona, and I appreciated her strong religious beliefs. We clicked instantly when she picked up on our mutually "normal" vibe. Sometimes we even went bike riding or to the beach just to talk as friends. With the stress of having the cameras constantly rolling, it was hugely important to team up with someone who let me be myself. We mainly talked about our significant others (my Nic and her Caesar), and ways to scheme moments of privacy with them that would preserve our love lives and our sanity.

In a way, Melissa brought out my good side when it came to communicating my love for Nic and the bad side when it came to pornography. Melissa believed that my high school attitudes toward women would never change. Everyone is entitled to their opinion, but it really hurts me when people like Melissa or old friends from Brooklyn who knew the misogynistic Joe refuse to believe that my attitude changed. The change began suddenly and unexpectedly, and I am sorry to disappoint a lot of people, but the boring truth is that I'm proud to be a churchgoing guy, who's committed to being true to love. I guess that image was too boring for Melissa to accept—or maybe she really did know something about Nic that I didn't know at the time and realized I was indeed being "played," so she wanted to encourage me back into the womanizing slump so I wouldn't get hurt. Who knows?

Melissa admitted getting a lot of pressure from home to live up to a certain standard, where the primary value was placed on being beautiful, making a lot of money, and maintaining a conservative demeanor. "Perfect, perfect, perfect." But that's the problem with appearances: they're about surface and not substance.

I think Melissa tried to protect herself by creating a false persona. She definitely had to deal with strict rules and regulations growing up Cuban and Catholic, but her family seemed more flexible, liberal, and lenient than any Catholic household I've ever encountered. She told me that in her family they openly talked about sex and pornography. I couldn't understand how that fit into her supposedly conservative lifestyle.

Melissa especially let down her guard on the computer. There's one specific episode where she's sitting at the computer, writing a cyber-sex letter. I don't know who it was to, but knowing her lack of discretion at the time, it could have been anyone. My guess is either one of the crew guys in the back office, or possibly Sarah's friend Hank from Wisconsin. You can actually see the letter on television. It says something like:

> You, me, and a lollipop, my beloved sex fiend. I was given a
> lollipop yesterday and as I ate it I got this crazy little idea. Will
> you share it with me? It doesn't have to be that big or even taste
> that good as long as we eat it together. How delicious. After you
> suck on it for a while, I hope you'll let your sticky saliva drip all
> over me. Will you spread this between my legs? I think you will.
> This is Melissa.

Hank probably thought Melissa really liked him. The way she talked to him, it would've been an understandable assumption. From my standpoint, they didn't just exchange sexy conversations, they covered a range of topics about their lives, too. Then, all of a sudden, Melissa just retreated and blew Hank off. Hank talked to Sarah practically every day over the phone, trying to find out what he had done to deserve Melissa's silent treatment. Sarah finally confronted Melissa and asked, "What's wrong with you?

You hurt his feelings," but Melissa, to my knowledge, never gave a straight answer.

Melissa got pretty friendly with a few of the camera and sound crew too, conversing via E-mail with them as well. Her closeness to them was one of the reasons she and Flora didn't come to the Bahamas with us, and how she found out what happened during my trip to New York, when I graduated and wound up getting engaged, before other members of the cast knew. It appeared that three crew members ended up getting fired for continuing to E-mail and communicate with her, ruining the dynamics of the household and compromising the integrity of the show. This was tried to be kept hush-hush, but it was so obvious to us. Many roommates resented her for being more friendly with the crew than with them.

Whenever Melissa felt pressured or unsure of her emotional state, she could run to her mother's house, since she was a Miami local. A couple of weeks before the filming ended, she just moved out, which was fine with us, but odd nonetheless. We didn't much trust her at all. When she couldn't face us anymore, she retreated. She said something on camera like, "They're not going to decide what I'm doing tomorrow. They're not going to make or break me. As you get older, you don't trust people as much." She seemed to have a lot of anger inside about something.

Flora and Flaunt-a

Flora created real problems for herself when she began dating Louis, her boss from the nightclub where she worked as a bartender. In something like the fifth episode of *The Real World,* I actually enjoy the way Flora and Louis's relationship is presented.

Walk This Way

When Melissa left the house prematurely, she allegedly took with her one of the house's most prized possessions: a photo of the housemates with Aerosmith's Steven Tyler. Among many other gripes, this had all the roomies p.o.'d. We happened to run into Steven on a random street in Miami. There he was, surrounded by tall, leggy blondes; and then there was us, ensnared by a camera crew. I suppose he only gave us the time of day because of the cameras—he's not one to pass up potentially free publicity, I'm sure, and probably wanted to maintain his good standing with MTV. He actually got along well with Sarah, and wondered if he could bring his kids over to check out our house and play with her someday (I'm guessing the kids he referred to didn't include his daughter Liv).

I took this opportunity to ask Steven what he felt was great about his life, only to receive a very common answer . . . that he has achieved happiness and comfort with himself *because* of himself, his way. Meeting Steven was an exciting moment for us all, but one we'll have to commit to memory, because Melissa allegedly took the photo off the fridge for herself and didn't bother to tell anyone.

It makes it look like Louis and Flora are going to be together forever; even if it's not the truth, it was really nice to see them so happy and compatible. TV editing does wonders and that "Maybe you're gonna be the one..." Oasis song closing out an episode as they walked on the beach together was touching.

As she was dating Louis, Flora simultaneously tried to sustain her relationship with her longtime boyfriend back in Boston, Mitchell. At its weakest, Flora's relationship with Mitchell was volcanic. I can't even describe the phone bills Flora ran up in conversations with Mitchell. Sure, our phone bills were huge because seven people shared one phone line—but Flora's share went on for pages and pages, calling Boston, Boston, Boston, Boston, Boston. It was unbelievable. She could've flown back and forth to Boston several times for the cost of her monthly phone bills. They hung up on each other a lot and she seemed to enjoy calling him back, continually leaving messages on his machine until he'd finally pick up again or she'd give up. It was funny to watch.

Flora's real trouble began one day while she and Louis were hanging out. She spotted Mitchell's jeep parked at the beach and knew Mitchell must have driven it down from Boston. That's when she knew she had some music to face.

Flora played up the Mitchell/Louis confrontation even more than it was portrayed on air. She exaggerated everything. She apparently gave Louis some lame excuse about needing to see Mitchell to end everything, and needed four or five days to let him down. Louis went along with it, although I doubt if he believed her.

I thought, Wow, MTV's providing a good service here by showing the bad judgment of one woman's search to control a relationship. Here's what happens when you're not honest with everyone involved. Flora seemed to have no intention of hiding the fact that she was involved with (at least) two guys at the same time. All the housemates knew she was headed for trouble, but she didn't want to hear it. She appeared to enjoy this kind of drama and chaos, getting herself into impossible situations to see if she could get out of them.

Every once in a while, some of us would try to give each other advice in the love department. Flora loved to counsel but rarely took advice. One time, however, she actually listened to us. It was the first time she really expressed how much she was in love with Mitchell and that her relationship with Louis was all a game. Getting her to sit down and actually talk about it was a miracle. She was really hurting. She never let people see her pain, but she wasn't putting up any fronts this time. She couldn't believe how straight we were being with her about her needing to be honest and make a choice between Louis and Mitchell. We definitely tag-teamed her on the advice.

Flora was lost somewhat like I was lost. Flora had difficulties with Mitchell in the way I had difficulties with Nic, and we both needed to admit the mistakes we'd made in our relationships. We discovered that we had this in common during one of the rare times that we actually spoke to each other. Like Flora and Mitchell, Nic and I pushed each other away out of insecurity and fear of commitment. Overcoming this fear is just the beginning of a solid, loving relationship.

For a club owner in Miami Beach, having MTV cameras around functioned as a good marketing device, but I don't believe Louis was looking for a long-term commitment with the show or Flora.

While I was in New York, graduating and getting myself engaged, Mike planned a surprise party for me. He also had the unfortunate pleasure of trying to extract money from everyone to help cover the expenses. Flora wouldn't go for it. Her attitude was that if Mike wanted to plan the party, Mike should pay for the party. She felt she had spent hundreds of dollars for other people, giving away free drinks to the roomies when they came into her bar, and she didn't feel obligated to pay a cent toward this party.

In her defense, Flora really hooked my buddies up when they came to visit me. She reserved a small downstairs area in the place where she bartended, pampering them with the VIP treatment all night, including a load of free drinks. She gave really hard-core discounts on everything, and was just being the nicest she'd ever been. I can't imagine how much money my buds would have spent had it not been for Flora's hospitality. I'm not sure what captured her interest and provoked her generosity that night.

Flora seemed to get along well with my buddy Serge. From the moment she hit it off with him, she decided my friends were really cool. I don't even know how this odd little connection started up, but I know that Flora is attracted to the masculine pheromonal discharge of money, which Serge did in large amounts. And I'm sure he gave her a huge tip. In general, Flora would do nice things for you if you did nice things for her first.

The Divine Miss Sarah

Sarah had relationship issues like the rest of us. She managed to keep her relationship with a guy back home extremely confidential. It didn't even come up during the show that she had a boyfriend. She never, *ever* talked about it explicitly because she didn't want to exploit it on camera. She'd joke that she was asexual. She did let me in on things a bit when she saw the difficulties I was having with Nic and wanted to help out. It seemed that she, too, had some serious problems with her love back home. I gather he hated MTV and the fact that she was in Miami. It caused her a lot of pain. He did call the house, but they never show it on camera, and if her relationship ever came up in discussion, she would make a joke and laugh it off. Generally, no one could ever get Sarah to be serious.

Sarah was on vacation for the entire five and a half months we were in Miami. She didn't have this big desire to develop close friendships with anyone while she was there because she was returning home to her great job. The comic-book company kept her on the payroll while she was in Florida, so she had total security. We were impressed by the fact that the company supported her during the *Real World* project and gave her assignments while she was there. She remained the editor of the comic book *Gen-13* while she was in Miami, and sent work back and forth via mail and computer, but it wasn't her regular full-time gig. They knew her awesome talents and didn't want to lose her.

In Miami, Sarah would mainly hang out with younger teenagers. She'd joke that the highest age group she was into was around sixteen. She didn't hide this at all. It was her thing, and she'd do her own thing always.

I admired Sarah for two major reasons—mainly, for saving my butt on the traffic corners whenever she dragged me out to Rollerblade, since we didn't have our own cars to do business-related stuff. And for being able to keep the whole experience in perspective for the entire five and a half months. It seemed she had no expectations when she signed on to do the show, partly because she planned to return to her job when the show ended, and also because she's not particularly materialistic. She never expected the business to make her a millionaire or even pay her bills. It really *was* like a five-and-a-half-month vacation for Sarah.

She never let the show get to her or reduce her to someone she was not. Others, like me, weren't self-aware enough yet to prevent this from happening.

Cyn

I remember when Cynthia verbalized her discontent because she felt the cameramen, the directors, and all the people behind the scenes weren't following her around like they followed the rest of us, and were therefore not getting her full story. I don't know the details, only that Cynthia was getting pissed about it. That was about the time she took a trip to Atlanta to see her mother and sisters and the cameras were fast on her tail.

It was when we saw this episode much later that we picked up insights into Cynthia we never would have known. In that episode, Cyn's mom didn't feel comfortable with outward physical displays of affection, like hugs and kisses, for Cyn and her sisters. Perhaps that's another explanation for why Cyn was so firm in her dismissal of the guys hitting on her. She'd say that she felt sorry for the guy who got involved with her because of her issues with intimacy.

Aside from a brief scene where Cyn harmonizes with her mom and sisters in Atlanta, the show doesn't focus on Cynthia's pursuit of a singing career. Cyn had the connections. She hooked up with this older entertainment lady in Miami Beach who knew all sorts of big-time rappers and producers in the music industry. She even sent Cynthia on auditions to try to get her some legitimate gigs.

I don't know who this lady was, but she was cool for Cyn. We all spoke with her when she came to pick Cyn up, because Cyn would generally take a long time to get ready. She regularly invited everybody from the house to attend various events, but I got the impression Cyn didn't want too many people from the house in on that·part of her life. One time they invited us to tag along when they visited a reggae lounge. I was the only one who went, and I ended up being the only white guy in the place.

At one point, Cynthia spent so much time with this woman, she began to feel isolated from the rest of the group. In the end, I guess nothing ever happened with her singing career. She did get close to being in some De Niro film, but who knows? *Real Worlder*s are infamous for getting close to things, but not many make it over that Machiavellian speed bump called typecasting.

Finding good and "real" lovin' in Miami was a challenge for everybody. Cyn, especially, avoided and refused any strong advances. Even the few guys she brought to the house who may have thought some kind of romantic thing was in the air soon realized she wasn't going for it. She had a man back home who treated her badly and never responded to her phone calls. He acted really nasty to her over the phone, which probably embarrassed her. That's one of the problems with long-distance relationships—if you can't communicate over the phone, you're doomed. Even when you are good at communicating, something special gets lost in the connection over the phone, especially if it's being recorded. It happened to most of us.

> *Life isn't about keeping score.*
> *It's not about how many friends you have*
> *Or how accepted you are.*
> *It's not about if you have plans this weekend or if*
>   *you're alone. . . .*
> *Life is about who you love*

And who you hurt. . . .
Only you choose the way those hearts are
affected,
And those choices are what life's all about.

—ANONYMOUS

We all made our choices in Miami, both good and bad ones. With those choices came consequences, and we've all had to deal with plenty of those: lost relationships; embarrassment to ourselves, our friends, our families, and in our workplace; financial strains and challenges related to the business; and much more.

CHAPTER FOUR

The Business

Big Ideas—and the One That Got Away

As the Miami cast of *The Real World,* we were given the unique opportunity to form a business with $50,000 in start-up capital. We were all to become equal shareholders in the company. MTV appointed Landon K. Thorne III, a Coral Gables business consultant, as our business advisor to help with logistical decisions, but other than that, it was up to us to figure out how to make a success story out of the $50,000. There weren't many rules, except that cash expenditures had to be checked by Landon, and the type of business had to be legitimate. We had twelve weeks to develop a solid plan and incorporate the business, or we'd have to forfeit the money and the opportunity. If everything went according to plan, the business was ours to take into the future. It sounded so simple.

Initially, I felt optimistic about our potential. The first few business meetings were full of excitement as we exchanged our visionary ideas. Everyone seemed so serious about getting something started, especially when Landon joined the group. At times, however, I wondered whether his role was to create unity or dissension. I never felt that he gave us the guidance we needed. After the first few meetings, disillusionment kicked in. Look closely at the first episode, and you can actually see the pain in our faces.

Generally, we started business meetings whenever everybody got home from work, aiming for five-thirty or six P.M. so that we could eat together afterward or I could barbecue.

My six business partners were entrepreneurs in their own unique ways. Sarah was the childlike entrepreneur: a free-spirited, anything-goes-as-long-as-I'm-happy personality. One of her visions was to open the largest skateboarding park in the world. Flora was the devious entrepreneur. Her vision was to open a "kick-ass" bar-cafe with all the trimmings and process the whole operation on a cash-only basis. Dan was a philanthropic entrepreneur. He envisioned an AIDS-free world of peace and happiness where an unthreatened rain forest would coexist in harmonious union with mankind (as long as it didn't interfere with his modeling career). Mike was the pyramid-scam entrepreneur. He envisioned a world of suckers who would buy whatever he sold because of his "selling" abilities. You could say that "Get the credit-card number and run" was an appropriate motto for him. Melissa and Cynthia had less definable entrepreneurial goals, but, at the very least, their spirits were fired with potential, not unlike the others.

I thought that the first few meetings should be devoted to establishing a strong level of trust between us and determining what each individual was good at, in order to build our business on that foundation. However, as things with Landon proceeded rapidly, we were asked to share our ideas before we even knew each other's personalities. We should have spent the first two weeks participating in some kind of team-building exercises—you know, things like the trust game, where you close your eyes and fall back into each other's arms, or a good paintball fight to break the ice. Anything to help us develop a sense of unity and trust in each other.

When we actually started sharing ideas, it was obvious that everyone had their own determined opinions, assumptions, and misconceptions about what was going to happen over the next five and a half months. No one—including Landon—understood specific expectations: what was required of the group, of each individual, or even of Landon. No one seemed to understand the basic philosophy behind teamwork or trying to make the business work toward the greater good. Most wanted to start a business primarily to make money, without having the slightest idea of what that meant, or that actual work was involved. There's no way a businessperson would ever choose a team like ours to work together. It was truly a setup for a breakdown.

All the optimism ended after the first week. In my opinion, the business collapsed the minute we walked through the door, and enthusiasm dropped even more every time Flora opened her mouth. She wouldn't even consider any idea other than her own. The only thing she wanted to do was open a coffee shop, and she laughed or grunted at other people's ideas or would say things like, "No way! I'm not here to do *that*! I'm not here to do a charity event! I'm not here to rent out bikes!" How can a group find common ground with attitudes like that buzzing around? Diplomacy rapidly became optional.

Between Flora's yammering and Dan's pontificating, the rest of us could've left the room for a week and they'd still have been hot-airing the place upon our return. One episode shows a typical session, with Dan rambling on and on. At this particular meeting,

Dan drove me to the breaking point. None of them knew me well enough to detect the warning signs. Whenever I become very quiet, stare at a fixed point, and lose my smile, that's a sure sign that I'm holding myself back and ready to explode. For better or worse, I couldn't hold it in anymore.

Judging by Landon's expression, he felt the same frustration, but didn't think it was his place (or politically correct) to interrupt Dan at the time. Members of the group warned, "Dan, this is a waste of time. You're talking in circles without listening to anyone else's opinion." Sarah tried to tap him and say something like, "Dude, you know, everybody's sleeping, it's obvious we need to stop here." But Dan felt comfortable in his own world. He insisted on reiterating the same point over and over again. Dan would be the first person to mock himself and his talent for rambling, but at this meeting he just wouldn't stop.

Finally, I decided to speak up. Through bouts of nervous laughter, I suggested we stop for the night because we weren't getting anywhere. When Dan tried to interrupt me, I challenged him to listen for a change. I knew other people in the group had things to say, but we were all exhausted. I couldn't believe that Landon didn't interject or guide our unfocused discussions. I guess he didn't think that was part of his job—or then again, maybe it *was* part of his job to let us all just explode for the cameras.

After I spoke up, Dan stormed out of the house and Melissa went after him. I don't know if she really cared how he felt, but I'm sure she knew the cameras would follow, and because of the high level of drama, the segment would probably wind up in the show—which it eventually did. Like most of us would on various occasions, she dramatized for the camera.

I knew Dan was upset with me and I wanted to clear the air. He felt pissed that I confronted him in front of everybody instead of taking him aside to talk. I told him that the meeting would have gone on and on and on and on for the whole night if I hadn't interrupted him. Eventually he was strong enough to take the constructive criticism and move forward, when Landon stepped in and spoke with him in one of those awkward one-on-one discussions. Dan respected Landon, and he responded well when Landon suggested that he try listening to his roommates instead of always trying to enforce his opinions and talk over them. Sometimes things just take a little more time and patience, of which most of the roomies, including me, had little.

Everybody came to Miami with some form of skill that could potentially benefit the group's business mission. I assumed we would evaluate what everyone brought to the table and go from there. I wanted to play a supportive role toward whatever business seemed most feasible, regardless of whose idea we followed.

Mike had an idea that, looking back on it now, could well have worked. He wanted to create a "Miami Beach Card" that would provide the holder with discounts to area businesses. He came up with financials and a general business plan, and he projected how and when we could be making profits. It all depended on how many cards we sold—we'd get out as much as we put in. It was a great idea that might have worked, but it wasn't glamorous enough for some, specifically Flora and Melissa, who weren't much into selling stuff. I didn't understand how the card would work at first. To be honest, all I could think about was the free multimillion-dollar international advertising and product exposure we would get by being on *The Real World,* and it seemed wasted on just a little card. I didn't really like the idea at all, but he did have a plan, and I realized its potential only later.

Typically, when someone had an idea, it meant a lot of work for the person who generated the plan while everyone else got a suntan, and this plan was no exception. The housemates loved attaching themselves to ideas that meant little work for themselves. They just wanted to sign the papers and let the business run itself, and usually, at least in the beginning, all the work landed on Mike and me.

The group's overtly passive attitude toward developing a business plan caused Mike to become despondent. He finally decided to quit working on his idea altogether when Flora and Dan began discouraging him. Frequently, when Mike shared his ideas, Dan would roll his eyes, and vice versa.

I suggested starting a business on the Web that would allow for all of our individualism to come out in full force: a personality-chat area on-line. This idea appealed to most, but still got the stink eye from Dan and Flora. Most ideas suggested by other group members were enticing at the outset, but they all eventually fell by the wayside. Eventually I began to think that Mike's other idea, to take the $50,000 to Vegas, put it on number seven, and let it ride sounded pretty good. It didn't quite cut it for the producers, though, like many others.

Trial and Error

Real entrepreneurs need to have a strong vision, be energetic,
and have a tolerance for risk. They must also have the vigor and
confidence to overcome the idea that they can lose everything
they own.
        —*my final MBA term paper*

This is how one of the coproducers summed up our business experience:

This generation complains quite a bit in print about the fact
they don't have the same opportunities that previous generations
have had, so we thought, okay, given this opportunity, let's see
what they do. . . . [The business angle also brought up] an issue
that's very interesting about this group and I think this age, and
that's the struggle with the concept of commitment. They were
at times afraid that any choice they made would define them for
life. They were very afraid to make that step because they
perceived it as *the* step into the adult world.
> —*Mary-Ellis Bunim to Karen Condor,* TV Host
> Weekly, *July 13–19, 1996*

Our personalities were so skewed and our visions so narrowly
focused that we could never fully please everyone in our group
within the twelve-week time period before we lost the initial
$50,000 investment (a capital limitation, indeed). In addition, cer-
tain members—the ones with the loudest voices—were too stubborn to see any direction other than their own. From brainstorm-
ing (forming) to verbal abuse (storming), we tried it all, with Joe
Cool, my Snoopy alter ego, at the helm trying to make sense of it
all. Joe Cool has never felt so ineffective as a manager. It was a
true example of managing chaos.

I struggled daily (being the designated leader most often in
communication with the investor) attempting to mold a vision
that satisfied the entire group. We'd present those agreed-upon
visions to Landon, who then made the appropriate amendments
and recommendations as dictated by the investor. By that time
the vision would no longer be ours. For example, my Internet
chat-page idea had every member of the group excited—at least a
little. The idea was severely amended by the investor because of
confidentiality issues: we weren't allowed to expose our identities

(so much for that multimillion-dollar marketing opportunity I was psyched about). The amendment to that idea came in the form of us having to use alter egos based on the demographics of the Miami area in order to move forward. This was by no means an acceptable vision to our stubborn group.

Landon K. Thorne, Guinea Pig

Landon regularly conducted private, seemingly impromptu meetings with each of us to discuss our feelings about the business, our personal lives, or anything else we could conjure up. I suppose he wanted to get to know us personally—or was required to get certain sound bites from us that he just hadn't been getting in the group settings. He also used these informal meetings as a means of relaying messages to us from the producers. Although he never really admitted that the producers were using him as a messenger, we could always tell something was up when he launched into a topic or line of questioning that seemed completely out of character for him, and harped on it for a ridiculous amount of time. Landon would say things like, "So, Joe, when Flora took off from the meeting, how did that make you feel?" He also had this terrible habit of mentioning the book he was writing, seemingly pretending I hadn't heard about it many times before. He tried to make the most of his camera time, I guess, like most of us did.

There were sides to Landon's character that were great, and sides that weren't. He was really cool when he supported our initial ideas early on, giving us immediate feedback, speaking from his heart. However, it was painfully obvious when Landon quit talking to us in his own voice and started channeling the producers'. I guess they got to him and chewed him up, telling him what he could and couldn't say to us. It seemed they made him change and retract certain promises and comments he made to us, and also made him agree to set up those individual conversations with each of us. If they needed specific footage or sound bites, Landon was the lackey to provide the right situation and commentary for them. In his defense, however, I recall a conversation with Landon in which he clearly stated how oddly his advisory status was being used by the show. *He* actually called himself a guinea pig like the rest of us.

I'm sure Landon may have wanted our individual meetings to be a time when we could sit back and let conversation and business productivity flow, but he always seemed to have a hidden agenda of topics to discuss. At times during certain individual and group discussions, he'd just happen to go in the back room (where the production crew was) for a little while and come out with a whole new perspective. I guess if he didn't know how the directors would respond or want him to react to something, he'd say, "Let me think about that and I'll get back to you tomorrow." Our "chosen" attorney seemed to operate under the same restraints. We couldn't get a straight answer out of the people who were supposed to guide us, because they were being dictated to by production. That's some business!

Landon's most memorable remark to me during one of our private conversations went something like, "Joe, you can take over the business and do it the way you want. Forget about the roommates. Roll with it and make money. They're just shareholders. You should be the president." I thought, what is he saying? This can't be right.

It turns out he said the same thing to Flora. One day, he called us into his office together and said something like, "Joe, Flora, why don't you just go for it together? Everything else will fall into place if you take the leadership roles."

Talk about a blow! Landon's suggestion for Flora and me to take over really distorted my feelings about correct business practice. I felt disappointed because I wanted to develop a real business with the guidance of a successfully established businessman. Landon would've been able to provide the kind of insight we would generally never have to work with at our age. Sometimes, however, his advice (which couldn't have been just *his* advice) was just wrong. It would have been nice for him to put us on track and put our interests above those of production. We needed to please the investor, sure, but not at the expense of creating a business we would all not be proud to own.

There was a time when Landon said something like, "Joe, you know I'm between a rock and hard place. I'm a guinea pig, just like you guys. I have to please all of you *and* the show's producers. This isn't normal for me. Sure, I had the knowledge and the advantage of getting my lawyer to do a lot of creative tinkering with my contract and you guys had to sign without making changes, but I'm still stuck in a position where I'm having to satisfy two seemingly *entirely* conflicting angles of the business, and that's not generally the role of a business advisor."

Mass Retaliation

About two months into the business discussions, I guess the producers were becoming concerned that everyone had taken on part-time jobs and we weren't fully focusing on the business, as required in our contracts. Landon pulled me away from the group for a private, one-on-one meeting. He gave me a message to relay to the rest of the group, basically declaring that they had to give up their part-time jobs and concentrate on the business. I didn't appreciate being the bearer of bad news, the scapegoat, the brown nose.

As suspected, this news didn't go over well with the group. They had bills to pay and couldn't afford to give up the part-time work. The kicker was that the only way we could get paychecks from whatever business we created was through *profits*. I don't know of many start-ups that see profits in the first five years, let alone the first five months. This became the majority of the group's first big reason for retaliation against the show. They firmly refused to give up their jobs, and there wasn't a thing the producers could do about it. I wish we'd had the luxury of not having to work; maybe we all would've been hungrier to get a business started if we could fully focus on it. But that's not the way it worked out.

Landon and I did agree on one element that's key to developing a successful business: An operating team needs to have a core philosophy, a core motivation, and a structured format to exercise that philosophy and achieve its goals. Partnerships or teams aren't built by using the dartboard approach. Landon fondly called several statements of this nature "Landonisms." A paperweight he gave me when the show ended reads, "Joe, Shine light into the dark corners and the ghosts will go away."

The Clothing Line

At some breakthrough point in our endless search for business opportunities, Dan stumbled across some designers looking for capital to develop a line of clothing. All they needed was the cash to get their label out to the public. Dan took Cynthia with him to meet the designers before he even proposed the idea to the rest of the group. He decided to represent us all and come back with a full report. This was a pointless interview, getting together with the designers without the whole group present. It represented another example of one roommate pulling a stunt that divided the group. The clothing line might have been the best idea in the world, but Dan was setting himself up for opposition by excluding us from his initial meeting. Maybe Dan had good intentions by delaying our introduction. Maybe he wanted to check out the designs before bringing us in to avoid wasting our time. I'd like to believe that, but his actions seemed selfish and, as he put it, covert.

As I saw it, the major problem with the clothing line wasn't even the huge risk and complexity of entering the world of fashion. My main concern was that the proposed modest line wouldn't create enough capital to build a larger business (and profits) fast enough for the rest of the group to stick with it. If we didn't make fast money, my business partners were sure to become discouraged and quit. But at the group meeting, when Dan told us all his idea, everyone seemed excited. Even Landon showed some enthusiasm.

The producers must have talked to Landon and told him to be strongly encouraging of this idea. From the show's point of view, a clothing line meant models, fashion shoots, Miami Beach haute couture, the hype of the fashion industry, and loads of great footage opportunities for the show. There's no question that the show, via Landon, wanted to plug this idea.

Not everyone in the house got into the idea. Sarah wanted nothing to do with the high fashion industry. Though we all worked a bit harder on the design idea, Sarah remained unenthused. She could've added so much to the idea. She even told

Landon about an idea for a bikini-bathing-suit line based on the designs in her *Gen-13* comic books. That was a great idea that would have fit perfectly into the fashion concept. But that's not what was in the mind of Dan or anyone else when it came to the fashion industry. They wanted high fashion, dresses, and expensive designs. Flora even broke from her coffee-shop fixation with a great idea for unisex overalls, which could've been a fast-selling fad item, but it was rejected by the "fashion elite" in the group.

Our first major responsibility was to draft a business plan. We divided the plan into seven sections and everyone was supposed to research and write up their specific part. I couldn't have made it an easier weekend assignment given the time constraints. I knew there wasn't enough time for everyone to conduct massive market research, but I hoped they would at least try to answer the questions to the best of their ability. I wanted everyone to be involved in the process this time. Ultimately, I used this project assignment as a test to determine whether or not we could all work together and make a business happen. When the assignments came back to me, the reality was quite negative. I worked my ass off to do my part and more, even through a difficult time in my relationship with Nic. Here I was, doing work for the business and work for my classes, and Nic was on the phone depressing me with conversations leading me to believe we were once again headed for a breakup.

I couldn't believe the final work that was handed to me when everyone completed their sections. Some pieces came back as just a page of complete baloney. Despite our last-ditch efforts, it appeared that we would miss the deadline to submit our business plan to the investors, thereby forfeiting the $50,000.

Fortunately, I suppose, the producers were true to their nature and considered drama more important than sticking to the terms of our contract. When the producers saw us pulling together to make the idea of a clothing line become a reality, they got excited and extended our deadline—big mistake.

When we missed the first extended deadline, the producers extended it again ... then again and again. I thought, This is ridiculous. We all needed the pressure of a deadline to get anything done, and the producers turned the deadline into a joke. That's when I decided to get out. So I scheduled a meeting with Landon.

Landon actually understood where I was coming from and admitted he felt the same way about the unlikelihood of the business ever becoming reality. When we were off-camera he somewhat admitted, "You're right, Joe! If I could, I'd get out of this, too. This whole experience isn't what I expected." He couldn't say much on camera that was anti–*The Real World*, but off-camera, he spoke honestly with me. He added, "When this experience is over, if you ever need money for a business opportunity, just let me know, and I'll help you out." I don't know if he said this to the other roommates, but it meant a lot to me then.

Attorney at Large

I made the suggestion that we use our attorney to assist in group negotiations and nagging. Sure, it would cost $175 an hour, but we needed a reality like that to cut through the garbage. Of course, Landon objected to this use of money, maybe because he felt threatened by our obvious need to hire someone to do the job we felt he should have been doing for us. I told Landon, "You don't understand! You're not here every day! You have no idea what it takes to motivate or get these people to make a decision!

Maybe if we pay an attorney 175 bucks an hour to provide some encouragement, the group will get off their freaking asses and do some work! It's time to light a fire and stop making excuses! Either we're here to create a business, or we're here for vacation. I'd like to know what we're here for, because either way, I'd like to start enjoying myself for a change."

Surprisingly, Dan had volunteered to find this somewhat affordable, decent attorney for us. This wasn't an easy assignment, but Dan emphatically took it on, assuring us that he would deliver. Unfortunately, when the deadline arrived, we were still without an attorney. Dan assured us he was assessing the situation, had narrowed down his selection to three lawyers, but he needed more time to arrange meetings for us to conduct interviews with them. Apparently, Dan hadn't seriously begun his search. With a little encouragement from me, he finally picked up the Yellow Pages and made a couple of phone calls. We interviewed and hired the first attorney he contacted that was "MTV approved"—you know, one who would actually allow cameras in.

As pleased as we were with Saul, our attorney, I think he became disenchanted with us. Seven people who are such a pain in the butt, sitting and arguing in your office, wasn't worth any exorbitant fee he could charge. Saul's fee was really the only non petty cash money we ever got permission to spend. Every expense was questioned, and I shouldn't have been surprised when I got a call from a director to verify the unwelcome fact that Saul's fee was even higher than the producers had expected.

I was asked, "Joe, how much did Saul originally charge you per hour? Was it $150 or $175?" I suppose they were trying to cut down his rate. I said, "Go back and look at the videotape. You've got everything on film, so there shouldn't be any discrepancy. I wrote down $175 but you can check it yourself." I hope Saul got some money out of the deal. He probably made more for a total of a few days' work than we brought home at the end of the five and a half months.

Check, Please

To do our part in getting our clothing business off the ground, Mike, Cynthia, and I decided to explore the Miami retail scene to find locations to sell our clothing line. I don't know what happened to Mike's enthusiasm, but he wanted to quit after walking only a couple of blocks. Maybe the parking meter expired, or maybe he thought, Why are we the only three out here looking for a location? It's not as if the rest of the group is back at the house drafting a business plan. They're all doing their own thing. This blows. Mike also needed money, and walking the streets looking for a mythical business location must have seemed aimless to him. Cynthia and I felt defeated. Mike had the car keys, so we called it a day. Nothing was coming fast enough for anyone in the group.

Soon after those pieces of a business plan came in from my roomies, like at the very next formal group meeting, I announced that I didn't want to continue in a leadership position. I was willing to do whatever work was expected of me, but I didn't want the leadership burden anymore. I said that I could provide input, wanted to help out, and would give up my shares, if that's what they wanted. I purposefully made it clear that I wasn't dropping out, just passing on the leadership baton. They didn't hear a word I said.

They all thought I had dropped out. I was trying to provide a chance for someone in the group to jump in and say, "I want to be the leader! I can do this!" But their reaction was a clear sign of the group's lack of ambition. Flora even admitted, "Joe, if you're not going to lead, it's over. I can't be a leader, I gotta follow. If Joe's out, I'm out."

I got choked up when she said that, though. I didn't expect her to react that way at all. I thought she would be excited by the opportunity. Flora had often maintained she wanted to be the president of our business, but she didn't want to be the leader. Funny, huh? She proclaimed

> An entrepreneur's home life may suffer as a result of the time they spend enveloped in their business dealings.
>
> —*my final MBA paper*

that she didn't trust anyone in the group to lead but me, and she assumed the rest of the group felt the same way. Sarah added: "I don't trust anyone in this house." (I think everybody said or thought that at one time or another.) I kept saying, "We can't start a business like this. You need to trust your business partners. We aren't just shareholders, we're partners, partners in business." The meeting ended in silence. I headed straight for the pool. I always went swimming in the pool when I wanted to refresh myself.

My greatest relief in stepping away from the leadership role in the business came in the form of kind words from my buddy Joonmo. He always seemed to be there for me during extremely rough times. He's a great listener and advice bearer. He has a certain presence that disarms people. For instance, when he came to visit me in Miami, he supposedly arrived at our house, opened the door without knocking, walked right in, and began shouting my name. No one was in the house at the time. As self-assured as he can be, I doubt he felt prepared for the emotional and physical mess he would find when he did see me.

I thought I would feel more freedom by letting go of my hopes for the business. Instead, I wanted to hide—just disappear from everything. But Joonmo wouldn't let me. I looked as nasty as I felt, but Joonmo wouldn't put up with my self-pity. He said, "Joe, if you're being honest with yourself and really thought the business was hopeless, there's nothing else you can do for your roommates." I couldn't understand why I didn't feel relief from stepping down or why I even cared about the group. He knew me better than I knew myself. He knew how much I cared and that I didn't want to leave my roommates stranded. Joonmo calmed me down and helped me relax. For the first time in two and a half months, I became more at home and at peace with myself. He helped me realize that I had made the right decision.

The more the group investigated, the more they realized how complicated it would be to learn the intricacies of the fashion industry. Time and enthusiasm continued to diminish and they began prowling around for a new

Dear Joe,

I just wanted to write you a quick note to let you know that I supported your decision about the business on the show. What a bunch of boneheads to have to work with. I most certainly would have done the same thing. I know you took a lot of heat from various people, but I just wanted to let you know that you made the right choice and that some people DO support you. I'm in a similar situation. I have just started my own business. BUT, I got lucky. My partners are absolutely great! Of course, I did get to pick mine. Anyway, good luck to you, man! I thought you were a pretty cool guy and I would have felt privileged to have you as a business partner.

— *another typical piece of fan mail*

idea. That's when Sarah's budding relationship with her new boss in Miami gave her the impetus to reintroduce the Delicious Deliveries concept to the group.

Delicious Deliveries

> [F]ocusing the energies and creative talents of these unique individuals would benefit both individual organizations and the world's business culture in ways that far outweigh the risks and costs of hiring independent-minded entrepreneurs.
> —*my final MBA paper*

Just when everyone had about given up hope on the business, Sarah came to the rescue. She had met a guy named Mark at one of Dan's *Ocean Drive* magazine events. Mark owned Hospitality Purchasing Network, a restaurant-supply business in Miami, and was looking to expand, but he didn't have the capital to do so. His new idea was called Delicious Deliveries and the concept couldn't have been simpler. Sarah described it as "home delivery of gourmet dessert treats."

Mark quickly stepped up to a leadership role in the group. He drafted a business plan, assigned job responsibilities to everyone, helped with legal issues, scouted locations, and did the rest of the unglamorous work that goes into establishing a company. It looked as if Mark just might save the day.

Shortly after getting the group into the idea, Mark pulled me aside and asked, "Joe, how did you deal with these people for so long?" Flora was back on her kick about being the president, even though she had admitted to being a follower. She rallied the troops to determine Mark's role and the percentage of shares that

It seems that many of my friends would like to get involved in a business with me. They have great ideas, but lack the drive to make anything happen (much like what you have run into on *The Real World*). It always ended up that I would do all the work and they would share in the profits. Needless to say, business relationships such as these rarely last. We can only learn from our mistakes and move on to more successful ventures.

—excerpt from a letter
from a current associate

he would receive if everyone agreed to invest in Delicious Deliveries. The concept was solely Mark's creation, vision, and dream, but Flora seemed to be scheming ways to take control over Delicious Deliveries, get most of the credit, and collect the greatest percentage of potential earnings.

In my view, now we were faced with an outside guy wanting to use our money and television exposure to further his own business goals. It's the exact situation I'd wanted to prevent from happening. I'd dreamed of creating a business that embodied our group passions—not funding someone else's.

Flora for President

The core problem with adopting Delicious Deliveries was that it wasn't our version of a dream business. The group planned to allocate 85 percent of the shares, and Mark could come in at up to 8 percent of that. The question was, which was more important to Mark: having the money or having the power in the business? The power was obviously the more important factor because of Flora's ambition. Mark wanted to be voted in as president of the company, since it was his idea, and Flora didn't want that to happen.

Once the group decided to go with Delicious Deliveries, Flora became Mark's shadow. She knew Mark was running the show and wanted to learn the ropes. Anytime Mark took charge and made a decision without consulting her, Flora didn't appear too happy. Sarah might have been the one to bring Delicious Deliveries into the house, but she didn't plan to stick with it once the show ended. She planned to return home and resume her job editing comic books. That left Flora in a great position to rally for control.

I decided to contribute my commentary on the situation by offering my shares to our dog Leroy, essentially making a mockery of the business. I quit taking the business concept seriously when our contractual twelve-week mark came and went and nothing had happened. That's when I finally started trying to enjoy my time in Miami.

The rest of the group actually started putting in some work for Sarah and Flora and Mark. They finally began to understand the pain and frustration of starting up a business. They figured out this wasn't a joke, it was a real business opportunity. It sure would have been great if they had known that before the twelfth week, instead of letting the opportunity just pass by.

Class Struggle

While the whole Delicious Deliveries scenario was working itself out, one of my professors, Professor Stoner, was giving me grief about not participating enough in his class. He accused me of not keeping up with the assignments. His class was the only thing standing between me and my MBA, and I certainly wasn't going to jeopardize missing out on graduation. I wasn't allowed many flights back to New York because the show had a limited budget and couldn't always afford to send a crew with me, and when I did make it to New York, it wasn't always on the days when class was in session. I had been E-mailing my professor constantly, sending him weekly assignments and status reports, providing him everything I thought we agreed would be required of me during the term. I made mayself believe that the only reason he called to threaten not to give me credit was because he wanted— or *expected*—to be on camera.

Professor Stoner needed to make sure I was keeping up with the class, so I did a couple of things. I began by setting up an on-line conference via my computer, connecting me with my classmates back in New York. I had my friend Serge on the classroom end, projecting the whole chat session onto a big screen while I spoke over a speakerphone. I orchestrated this whole session to demonstrate to my professor that I was doing what I could to fulfill his curriculum requirements despite my unusual circumstance.

Initially, Professor Stoner was flexible and accepting of a cyber-class structure, and we agreed on a plan that included videotapes of the class, E-mailed assignments and conferences, faxes, and phone conversations. Other classmates kept in touch with me the same way. I probably conversed with them more than I would have if I were physically in class everyday.

I got the feeling from various classmate E-mails and my own conversations with Stoner that he just wanted to bust my chops and make sure I was doing the work and he was being extra tough on me because, when we made the deal, he expected to be on-camera. To my knowledge, my classmates never complained about my participation and didn't think I was getting special treatment just because I wasn't physically in class every day. But when Stoner called and told me he wasn't in a position to give me

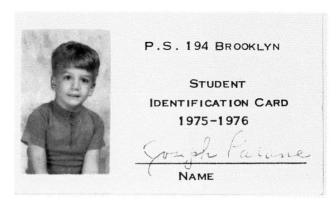

P.S. 194 BROOKLYN

STUDENT
IDENTIFICATION CARD
1975-1976

NAME

It all started pretty casually in kindergarden . . .

. . . but continued in a
fourth-hand uniform at
Good Shepherd
Elementary School.

Mom and Pop happily honeymooning in St. Mark's Square, Venice, Italy, 1954.
Before the eight kids came along.

Helping Nic blade through the streets of New York City. I really miss that.

"So, you're leaving me. . . . Let me cook you something nice . . . heh, heh, heh."

Me and the *real man,* Kenneth, on Happy People Marina in the Bahamas. I think the marina must have been named for him.

My favorite thing to do in Miami Beach: barbecue!

Joonmo and me chillin' in the pool behind the house.

Nic and me vacationing on the California coast
after she'd returned from Italy.

Nic and me dressed
up in matching suits
(she's wearing the
pants). Check out
that rock on
her finger!

The phone at Walgreen's. Was no place safe?

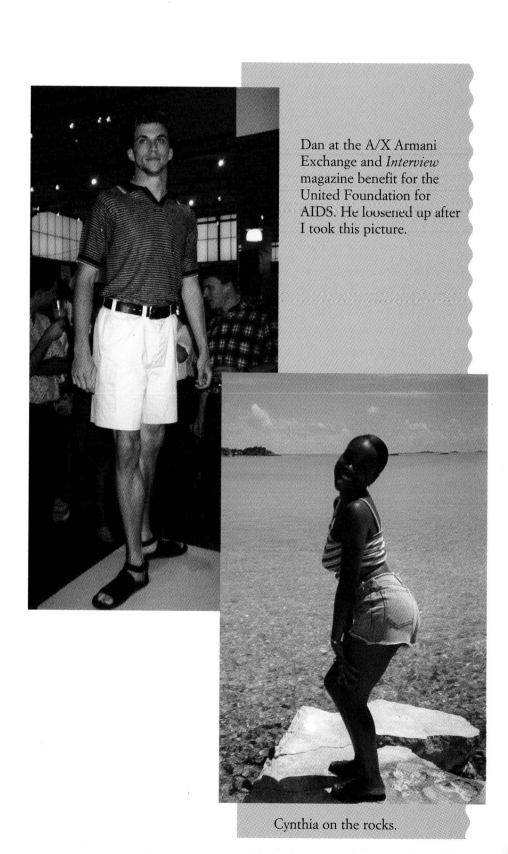

Dan at the A/X Armani Exchange and *Interview* magazine benefit for the United Foundation for AIDS. He loosened up after I took this picture.

Cynthia on the rocks.

Flora and Melissa. Let's just leave it at that.

Hard at "work": Mike on his IBM and me on my Apple eMate.

Steve Wozniak (Woz), cofounder of Apple, models his stylish, multicolored, collapsible, wraparound sunglasses. His suggestion that the roommates start a business selling these sunglasses (and their fashionable necklace carrying pouches) came a little too late.

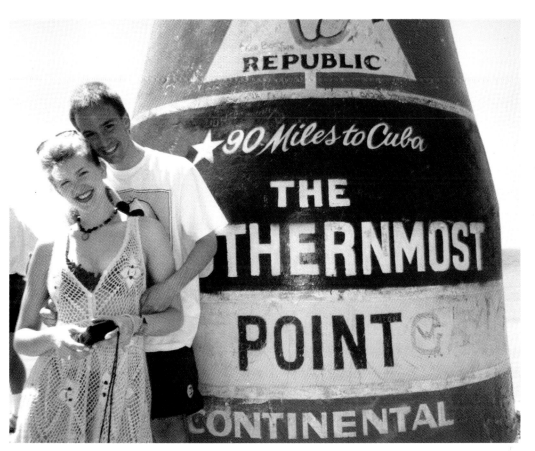

Our Key West getaway vacation.
We couldn't get any further away if we'd tried.

Mike, Sarah, and me on a speaking tour at a college after the show ended. I'd been
out of touch with them (and the world in general) for a while,
trying to make sense of what was happening to me.

First draft of the book manuscript . . . done!

The Multiple Sclerosis Bike Tour benefit in New York City. I had no idea what a long, painful, lonely ride was in store for me.

Snoopy, my sis Christina, and me in the early years.

Me and my newly repaired VW bug (thanks, Ralph!) after the car crash during my freshman year of college.

My parents, Joonmo, and me at my nephew Christopher's Christening
(that made nine . . . and counting!).

Mike and me behind the scenes at the wrap party. I'm all wet because the
crew had thrown me in the pool, and Mike must be stunned seeing the
room full of camera equipment that had been recording our every move
for the last five and a half months

Dan and Arnie, Nic and me—*classic*.

a grade for his class, I knew I had to make a special trip back to New York to ensure getting my credits to graduate on time.

I teamed up with a classmate, Cordell, who wanted to help me out, and we worked together on-line to devise a class presentation. The plan was for me to arrive in New York unannounced and blow the class away with this presentation. Cordell's helping hand really kicked!

This showdown with my professor occurred during the last week of class. Maybe the directors were looking for a little drama and called my professor to light a flame under my butt, but that's complete speculation.

When I walked through the door, I felt as though Professor Stoner was happy to see me—and the cameras. I was pleased with the way our presentation (entitled "Balance Through Personal Leadership," based on the book *First Things First* by Stephen Covey) turned out, and so was he; that's all that counted. I curiously ended up getting an A in his class. Considering that I was supposedly "failing" the week before, I felt that our presentation must have been quite accomplished. Maybe my professor was trying to help me. I blamed myself more than anyone for the business failing, because I was the guy with the business background. I was supposed to have the know-how and motivational skills to create teamwork in the most extreme situations. But nothing I did, not even the Myers-Briggs type exercise I initiated, seemed effective, and the group remained unresponsive to my encouragement. The same held true when Sarah and Flora tried to take the reins. Momentum for Delicious Deliveries disappeared when, as another class excercise to show my professor the pains I was going through, I had the coordinating producer personally videotape a meeting in which I confronted my roommates about how they were living out Mark's dream business and not their own, certainly discouraging them from continuing on that path. It obviously worked, but nothing took its place and the business side of things was unofficially finished.

The Keys to Paradise: A Respite

Before the business officially ended, production sent us on a weekend trip to a secluded island in the Bahamas. Cyn was completely hungover when we boarded that twin-engine plane to the Exuma Keys. We got the pilot to do various dips just to aggravate her nausea. It was just enough to get Cyn puking into a bag during the flight. It was pretty funny, but pretty gross. Certain of us wanted the pilot to perform tricks over and over again so Sarah could take more pictures of Cyn puking.

When we landed, Kenny, a multi-award-winning sailing champion, greeted us and introduced himself as our host on the one populated island we stopped on before boating to our destination island. He was *the man* on the keys. He knew everything about these islands and how to survive there. He's the one who introduced me to conch, which is now one of my favorite shellfish. Restaurants served conch all over Miami, but I had never harvested it from the ocean or watched it being prepared—it's not a popular activity around my neighborhood in Brooklyn. After only a couple of hours on the populated island, we were sent off on a boat to our secluded island.

When we jumped off the boat and waded to shore, the only things we could see on shore were three tents and some recreational items—sailboats, scuba gear, and so on. We let Dan have his own tent, which he didn't seem to mind. Mike and I, and Sarah and Cyn, shared the other two. Although we were on a deserted island, we weren't exactly roughing it—no cracking open coconuts and diving for oysters here. We had a specialty chef, Blake, who was on call to feed us meals and snacks throughout the day. She made the most amazing food with extremly limited equipment.

The island was paradise in every way but one—too many bugs! And I mean like, *Hoo-aa!* Big-ass bloodthirsty bugs! We sprayed bug repellent on everything but the food. They supplied us with an extra-strength formula, but that didn't stop these suckers from coming after us at all.

I was exceedingly pumped to be out of Miami, needing a break from its artificial environment. A couple of weeks earlier I had mentioned that I had never been full scale camping and couldn't wait to try it. I envisioned my first experience to be exactly like this trip. Until I tried to sleep on that first dreadful night.

It was so freakin' hot I couldn't breathe inside the tent. It was hotter inside the tent than outside. I saw some of the crew sleeping by the ocean (they had their own tents pitched hundreds of yards away), so I tried to do that, but there were too many of those darn bugs. I was dying! As beautiful as this place was, I got very little sleep there. Dan, on the other hand, had no problem, sleeping in his own tent. Every morning, I'd walk up and down the shore, just thinking, waiting for everybody else to wake up.

Every night I was so tired from swimming all day that I didn't even want to talk. All I thought about through dinner was, When are we going to bed?—until I got into the tent and realized I wouldn't get any sleep anyway. I actually longed for the house bed, not knowing that Leroy the dog was wreaking havoc on it with my chewing gum while we were gone.

There was no alcohol on the island. Then again, maybe the crew had some, probably more than we'll ever know, but we didn't have it or need it. The five of us who had chosen to come were totally chilling, getting to know and enjoy each other's company. We were going through a challenging experience in Miami, so it was nice to share this time away. The four days gave us plenty of time to focus on a level we never would have reached amid the distraction of everyday life and Miami, kind of like a retreat. We took advantage of that beautiful environment, feeling grateful that Flora and Melissa hadn't made the trip. It seemed they had their own agendas that definitely didn't include camping or getting to know the other roommates.

We soon found out that if you had to go to the bathroom, it was best to use the ocean. Believe it or not, we were told by our guide, Barty, that this was the most environmentally friendly option, as long as you went really far out from shore; the tiny Porta Potti thing was clogged up all the time anyway. Cynthia was mortified. I wouldn't be surprised if she held it in the whole time.

Barty stayed mainly with Cynthia to ease her stress about being on the island, while the rest of us just chilled. It was the most incredible experience I ever had—swimming, snorkeling, and sailing in crystal-clear water. I continually imagined spending my honeymoon with Nic on this island, as I'd just gotten engaged to her the week before.

I especially loved the snorkeling. We practiced in a shallow area to learn the basic technique, then headed out to a reef. The fish, the coral, the plants—there was so much to see. Sharks were all over the place, too. We saw a few from the boat along with some stingrays. We swam with Barty into this incredible cavern where beams of sunlight streamed through a crevice at the top. I never experienced anything like it—it felt very spiritual, like being in a cathedral.

Another big activity was sport fishing. I caught the most beautiful fish that struggled as I tried to free it from the hook. The fish kept holding on. It wouldn't let go and it was dying! I thought it wouldn't make it. Miraculously, however, Dan freed the beauty and it swam back to freedom. For some reason, I saw this whole ordeal as a lesson in relationships. The place was constantly provoking deep thoughts like that for me. It was a tropical paradise of wisdom.

The Final Hour

As we neared the extended deadline for turning in a business proposal, having rejected every possible backup plan, Flora's coffee-shop idea resurfaced. This time, everyone showed signs of wanting to be involved, so we went in search of a location.

Eight days before doomsday, Flora, Saul, and I scouted a place for sale called Ali Baba's. The owners agreed to sell us the place and everything in it for exactly $50,000. Coincidence, or what? The lease included everything in the place—furniture, kitchenware, cash register, towels, everything. The cafe appeared to be in good shape, in a location perfect for attracting South Beach traffic—exactly as Flora had envisioned. It was enough to respark my interest in fighting for the business.

Landon worked the investors and told us that if we needed a little more money for an even nicer place, it could be arranged. For the fashion-industry project I had asked for a quarter of a million dollars, and Landon had made it seem as though that wouldn't be a problem, so I projected big investment potential into this place. I was sure this was a cash-cow possibility for all if franchised, and an interesting business venture to portray on the show.

Toward the end of our time in Florida, Sarah distanced herself from working on the business, but Mark still wanted to be involved. He saw the potential for Delicious Deliveries to operate from the coffee shop, so he and Flora began strategizing together. It wasn't long before Mark realized working with Flora basically meant having to do most of the work alone . . . again. Starting the coffee shop meant having to rewrite the shareholders' agreement and the business plan, and rework the numbers.

At this point, however, Sarah was looking forward to returning to her job in California, Dan was planning to model in Italy, Cynthia had just landed a full-time job in Miami, and Melissa was back in the safety of her parents' home, leaving an unenthused Mike, Flora, Mark, and me (via Leroy the dog), to run the coffee shop.

It looked like we might pull off the impossible in the final hour, but Dan was in charge of securing the lease for an even better location we'd found, yet disappointingly, he didn't. His preoccupation with *Ocean Drive* magazine and the modeling scene was his downfall. Everyone got caught up in something Miami had to offer.

With that, we officially lost another real opportunity to make a go of a business in Miami. But the fault didn't come down to one person. We all have to take responsibility for blowing the opportunity and the $50,000. It's as if we actually did go to Vegas, put the whole wad on number seven—and lost. It just took a little longer, and was a lot more painful with the route we took. (A map surely would have been helpful here.)

Sarah and I wanted to realize our dreams with or without the opportunity to realize a profit. We just wanted to make a difference and teach the world that anyone can build a business with energy and grit. And the constant interference from the production company didn't help matters much. Had we been allowed to communicate with the investors directly, we would have realized the undoables ahead of time and focused on the "reality": that the interests of the investors (MTV Networks and Bunim-Murray Productions) via Landon were much more important than our own.

I took the whole business venture as an exciting challenge from the start, but it turned into a burden that unbalanced my personal and professional life. The Miami life was overwhelming, and I found that I needed to refocus on what was real and important to me. In so focusing, I managed to get out of the business, get my MBA, and get out of that unreal town called Miami Beach before it got the best of me—but you know, come to think of it, it sure would've been nice to buy my dad a cup of coffee in my own cafe.

CHAPTER FIVE

Nic

In a dream, my love,
you will find my heart.
>   —*I wish I wrote that, but it's from some song*

Love at First Chance

’m five foot six, which wouldn't be remarkable until you saw me standing next to my six-foot girlfriend, Nic. *The Real World* executives loved that Nic was an attractive model who towered over me both physically and emotionally. Whenever the camera was on us, we operated on two plateaus—nauseatingly lovey-dovey, or intoxicatingly venomous. When we weren't holding hands, baby-talking sweet nothings to each other, we'd be arguing about whatever hit a nerve at a particular moment. Our conflicts would lead to passionate reconciliations or silent treatment and separation. The trial of having a camera constantly around us certainly heightened the intensity of our emotions.

We Meet

I spotted Nic working at the gym in the building where I lived as a resident director at Fordham. She'd come in and out of the Residential Life Office to drop off the gym keys at opening and closing time. I became mesmerized by her smiling face and elegant style every time she stopped and joked with me. But our transient interaction was limited to innocent flirtation until the day she seriously considered joining my dorm softball team. From that point on, I was smitten. Unfortunately, however, toward the end of that summer semester, she informed me of her plans to visit and work in Italy and said she would say good-bye before she left. I came back from class one evening and found a note under my door that read, "Stopped by, but you weren't here."

A year and a half later, Nic resurfaced. I walked out of my office, and there she was—standing at the dorm security desk in this sexy pink outfit, wearing sunglasses, looking all hot and high and mighty. She was using the desk phone to call her friend upstairs. I was frozen with excitement, but didn't think she'd remember me. I felt kind of small, so I pretended to have some important resident-director business to do behind the security desk. Nic didn't say a word, so I retreated back to my office.

About twenty minutes later I saw her pick up the phone again and knew she was planning to make her move upstairs, so I decided to head her off, aiming for the elevator, praying we would ride up together. Finally, as she approached, she recognized me, made the connection, and exclaimed, "Oh my God! Hi! I just came back from Italy! I have to show you all the pictures of the modeling work I did!" Somehow, I was able to think over my boisterously beating heart, *Thank God! She remembers me! I was so psyched!*

She coaxed me off the elevator and into her friend's room (who wasn't home yet). We sat on a bed and went through her modeling book. I felt totally uncomfortable and invited her up to my place where I would feel more relaxed. After a little explaining about the rules forbidding me from being in a female undergrad's room alone, and a bit more coaxing, she agreed.

We planted ourselves on my couch and after just a short period of small talk I said, "I really want to kiss you. . . . May I kiss you?" She replied, "Yeah, I've wanted that, too." The rest was history.

From that point on, we hung out constantly for months. We worked together, played together, communicated, yet still gave each other space to do things separately from the other. It was amazing to be so productive, so free, and so in love with someone. She understood my endless hours working at the computer, and my hyperactive need to go play outside once in a while. I didn't think about anyone else. To me, she was the complete package, beautiful inside and out—the ultimate woman. But she certainly wasn't easy!

Bringing Me to My Knees

Unlike several former female companions, Nic didn't like to be "on a leash"—she wouldn't come when I wanted her to come, she wouldn't stay when I wanted her to stay, she'd bust my chops night and day making me wonder what she was up to. She thought for herself and challenged me and my thoughts. This took some getting used to, but I liked it! We grew deeply comfortable with each other over a short but intense period of time.

I've generally attracted supportive girlfriends who encouraged me to follow my super-achiever goals, no matter how crazy they sounded. They kept me out of trouble, away from distractions and focused on my work, and were always at my beck and call. My life became their life, but not vice versa— which was a major source of my relationship issues. Whenever I needed anything, they would deliver—if I wanted Italian food, we ate Italian; if I wanted to watch a Disney flick, we'd rent one; if I was frisky, we'd get frisky. This was not the story with Nic. Nic was the most stubborn woman I'd ever encountered. She challenged me every day of our relationship, and gave me a crash course in how to treat women with respect.

I've never seen Joe so vulnerable. He doesn't like to drink because he doesn't like to be out of control. Nic brings out a side of Joe that makes him weak. Before he met her, Joe never saw his own dark side. He's making a big effort to change his sexist attitudes toward women. She's a big part of the process for him.

—*Joonmo Ku, my bud*

I think it's beautiful to be in the kind of love that makes you feel indestructible and powerless at the same time. For me, Nic radiated beauty from her heart and made mine swell with joy. I was putty in her arms.

I really gave in to something with Nic that's difficult to explain. It's the kind of love that brings a man to his knees. That's something I never experienced before meeting Nic—letting go of my need to lord over women and being able to trust that I wasn't at risk of losing my own identity. As my friend Sue Dean said, "I think any kind of love that brings you to your knees brings out some hidden good things and some hidden junk that you never knew you had."

Down in Miami ... for the Count

Before I left for Miami, I was in true romantic bliss. I considered no one capable of measuring up to Nic. I probably didn't make this clear enough to her, or perhaps she just didn't understand the fact that I really needed her, wanted her, and felt invincible with her by my side. I was afraid of these feelings and communicating them at this incredibly exciting time, but I definitely would have given up the *Real World* experience and stayed in New York if she had sincerely asked me to—for better or for worse.

> When I first met Joe, I thought he was so nice. And my friends were flipping out because I never said a nice thing about a guy until I met Joe. I couldn't stop telling them how he was intelligent, spiritual, and trustworthy. They thought we would be together for a while.
>
> —Nic, in an interview

Before I left, we were a loving, caring, sharing couple. But that all changed shortly after I arrived in Miami. I could tell over the phone that something was wrong. She wasn't responding in a familiar way; she seemed reserved. I knew something or some*one* else was on her mind.

My whole relationship with Nic became really twisted once my roommates got involved. The cast loved her in the beginning, although I sensed some jealousy of her good looks when I circulated pictures of her. Dan jokingly admitted being jealous that she had me, instead of his having me. In one episode he's seen coveting the phone with her on the line; after Nic impatiently asked to speak to her man, he said, "He's mine, now." (Unfortunately, however, Dan's just not my type.) Then, two months into *The Real World*, when Nic and her friend Julie came to Miami, things turned exceptionally bad.

On the day Nic was scheduled to arrive in Miami, I was foaming at the mouth and sweating profusely as I ran through the airport from terminal to terminal with her favorite frozen yogurt I'd bought for her dripping down my arm.

When I finally found her gate, she seemed so happy to see me. But there was something pensive about the expression on her face. I knew her well enough to detect that something was wrong. Then I noticed a hickey on her neck. She laughed it off and told me her friend Julie gave it to her as a joke. I laughed it off, too, determined not to start an argument. I was just so excited to see her. But the peace between us quickly disintegrated as the reality sunk in: the cameras had been on me, even as I raced through the airport, and were certainly not going to leave me alone, especially with her in town.

I wanted my roommates to get to know Nic better, especially since I'd have to listen to them bitch about her afterward if they didn't like her. I hoped Nic would suck it up a little, put forward a sincere but brave front, and help me deal with the camera and

I knew things were getting tough for Joe in Florida when he started fights for no reason over the phone. He'd get a little pissy, because things weren't going well. He had a lot going on. He didn't vent or talk to me about the problems. He had a lot of frustration, feelings of anger. They frickin' did a job on him. We never yelled at each other, or even raised our voices to each other, until *The Real World*.

—Nic

roommate situation for a few days. This is how I dealt with many facets of her being in the modeling industry that I didn't necessarily feel comfortable about, but I did it for her.

Unfortunately, however, the minute Nic walked through the door of the MTV house, she did a lot of complaining. I knew she felt uncomfortable staying at the hotel on the beach I'd set her up in, but she went into extreme detail with every one of my roommates about all the hotel's flaws. She told Cynthia that her mom would never let her stay in this kind of place, then detailed a cockroach sighting to Dan. She complained about the toilet to Flora. It wasn't exactly the way to win over any of my roommates' affections, let alone mine.

One of Melissa's reactions to Nic was plainly "Joe, you're getting played." She thought Nic was dragging me along for the ride, getting me to do whatever she wanted, so she could share part of the MTV spotlight. To some extent, I felt she might have been right, but I didn't care. I thought I loved her and wanted to work for a balance in our relationship.

> Joe made me feel really uncomfortable with [his roommates] when I went to visit him in Miami. Joe tried to play Cynthia and me up against each other. He told me that she was trying to make out with him, she was coming home drunk and trying to "go with him." She tried to make out with him three or four times. How was I supposed to feel?
> —*Nic*

I admit to playing this game to provoke a jealous reaction, or any reaction, from Nic. I wanted her to want me more than she acted like she did when she was in Miami. If Nic had really wanted to be with me, she could have stayed with me in Florida.

Modeling offers the flexibility of finding work almost anywhere in the world, including Miami. As she put it herself, she's a model, she can get work anywhere, and she wasn't committed to any schedule. But I guess she wasn't ready to make a commitment to me, especially while other men were waiting in the wings for her as usual.

Generally speaking, Nic and I were pretty mushy with each other whether or not the cameras were rolling. We received plenty of flak from friends and strangers about our baby talk, but that was a cute way she and I liked to communicate. I felt like Nic was the only one I could talk to when I was freaking out about the show. But it turned out that Nic clearly wanted me to go to Miami so she could have freedom to do her own thing, date other guys, whatever. She was feeling too much for me and that stressed her out. She wasn't capable of being there for me, let alone communicating to me over a phone line when every word was recorded.

At one point, I really wanted Joe to go to Miami. I remember telling my two best friends that I hoped Joe would go with someone else while he was in Miami so that I wouldn't feel guilty. I was feeling too much for him, and thought, Holy shit! This might work! I was seeing somebody else at the same time. All he did was talk about money. Joe wasn't like that. Joe was Mr. Computer Guy, so calm, intellectual, nice, and quiet, working on his master's degree . . . then the whole MTV thing swallowed him alive. Joe got pushed into this superficial world down there, and it naturally rubbed off on him.

—*Nic*

Nic turned out to be in about eight episodes of *The Real World*. The directors even individually interviewed her on camera whenever they got a chance. After watching the shows, we began to feel as if she was an actual cast member. Often, she received more on-camera time than other members of the house. When she signed the release form, she assumed she would have a minor role, but things got out of control as the shows were being edited, I guess. It became a nightmare.

Trust Me

Nic had issues with me being in Miami primarily because she couldn't keep an eye on me and just plain didn't believe in me. I didn't go out once during the first two weeks, but Nic innately assumed I'd be up to something. Instead of constantly going to nightclubs with my new roomies, I stayed in the house doing my own thing—sorting all of my paperwork, putting together photo albums, working on my computer with business or class stuff, taking care of the finances, you name it—while everyone else soaked up the South Beach life. I wanted to be alone with my thoughts at the time, not hang out with the group. I didn't know my roommates or feel comfortable with them yet. It was easier for me to be faithful to Nic by avoiding the nightlife scene altogether. Being a nondrinker and a nonsmoker, I never much got into the allure of the bars and nightclubs anyway. Nic was the same way, I thought.

> I never imagined I would be in more than one episode of *The Real World*. I didn't apply to be on this show, I wasn't made aware that this was a possibility of what they could do. Joe's the one who went for this, not me. It became a nightmare.
>
> —*Nic*

Losing Faith

I'll never forget the phone call when I asked Nic if I should worry about her dating other guys while I was away. She nonchalantly said, "You don't want to know." I also remember the "don't worry about me, don't worry about me, just do whatever you need to do" conversation. That really hurt me.

Nic's attitude was, "What am I supposed to do? Sit on my ass and wait around for Joe to come home?" Well, yeah, that was the general idea, I thought. One night, I called her house and her father answered the phone. When he heard my voice, he said, "Oh, is this [insert another guy's name here]?" I told him, no, it was Joe, but the damage had been done. I was crushed. My suspicions were confirmed, so I started seeing other women.

I never felt as though I had failed in my life until I found out that Nic had been seeing someone behind my back. I thought, How could this be true? I'm Joe Patane, the guy who dated five women simultaneously in high school, who all knew about each other and that I wouldn't commit to any of them. I'm *Joe*, the so-called "guy who had two prom dates." Girls don't cheat on me, I'm in control here. My ego got so hung up on itself that I acted like a big fool. "Go to Miami," Nic suspiciously encouraged. She told me not to worry.

Supposedly, Nic dated other guys before and after I was on the show, supposedly because she loved me too much and didn't want to fall in too deep with me. When I woke up to this, I started dating. Somehow, Nic decided *my* dating outside of our relationship was far worse because I did it on camera, failing to factor in how I never would have started dating other people if *she* had been faithful. See where this is going? It's an endless, tedious cycle and still comes up in arguments to this day.

Gone Astray

After I confirmed Nic's involvement with others, I started seeing
Leah. We went out off and on, until Leah just wouldn't go away. I
never gave her my phone number, but somehow she got it from
her friend Tara, who knew the previous tenants of our house. Tara
called and asked for me and I hadn't even hung out with her. To
this day I believe this whole situation may have been "production-
ally planned—you know, an MTV setup.

The next thing I knew, in one bold and somewhat presumptu-
ous move, Tara and Leah were riding up to the house on Wave
Runners, along with a bunch of guys. I had Flora do what she
does best and scare them away. She was happy to oblige. I meant
to send a message that said, Don't let that happen again. I didn't
want to get too close to Leah. I was really just upset with and
missing Nic, weak and hurting.

Over a month passed, and Nic was still dissing me over the
phone. Simultaneously, Leah would get in touch with me just to
hang. Hanging out with Leah meant getting away from *The Real
World* house and roomies for a welcome bit. Most times, all we
did was talk and watch television at Tara's fiancé's place with
Tara—something I wasn't allowed to do in the MTV house
because of the sound restrictions. It became my oasis from the
house, where the business and Nic were driving me crazy. I told
Leah everything about Nic, and made it clear that my love for Nic
was exclusive. But Leah had apparent hard-core feelings for me.
At one point, she even told me that she loved me. That comment,
for some reason, made it to the air. Whatever! I thought, What,
are you kidding me? You don't even know me!

Because we were hanging out so much, I did some hand-holding
and kissing with Leah, but I thought those insignificant times were

all off-camera. We were walking together one night, talking about relationships, and it felt good to be with someone who seemed to understand my situation better than Nic. I made myself believe the cameras were nowhere in sight. We reacted to the moment and kissed. A camera straggling somewhere off the road or in a van many yards away had zoomed in and captured that kiss that made it to the air.

> He swore that the cameras never caught him holding hands, kissing, or touching anyone. . . . Later I found out more about another girl, then another. That really bothered me. I couldn't believe he would do that to me.
>
> —*Nic*

The work I put into believing in Nic from the outset wasn't reciprocated. That's very difficult to accept, but I should have realized her lack of faith in me earlier. I actually feel foolish that I didn't work harder at our relationship, but the realities were quite overwhelming so I tried to escape. Nic hated feeling out of control or vulnerable, and our relationship made her nervous, because I seemed to provide everything she was looking for in a partner and vice versa. She thought, Something could really work out with Joe, and felt justifiably frightened.

We dated others out of spite and anger, but we were both just fooling ourselves. To me, no woman compared to Nic. I wanted her in my life and I realized that even more when I was with someone else. It was never truly revealed on the show that Nic was dating other men, which made me look like the big jerk. She seems to think it makes her look like a loser for being with me at all. Every time MTV interviewed Nic on camera, they tried to pry the stories from her. But she wouldn't break under their interrogation. Her answers were always diplomatic, like "I think Joe needs to concentrate on himself." They interviewed her for many hours at a time.

Toward the end of filming, Nic and I tried to clear the air, admit to our exploits, and move ahead with some truth and dignity. No surprise, Nic had lied to me about the hickey, and it all came out as we confessed our infidelity. But despite all of the emotional damage we caused to each other, I still felt she was the one for me and I wanted to marry her.

I feel Nic's pain now. I couldn't believe she would do to me what I was doing to her and I can't imagine what it would be like to see it on camera. I hurt myself in hurting her, and I can't apologize much more than I have. I really messed up. Being referred to as *the man* is not cool to me anymore. It's foolish.

> *Brandon:* I can say I'm sorry over and over again, but it won't take back or make better what I've done to you. I know now what it means to do the time.
> *Kelley:* How would I know it wouldn't happen again?
> *Brandon:* You wouldn't, it's just a leap you'd have to take . . . I can't take it for you.
> —Beverly Hills, 90210, *February 4, 1998*

Nic

The Proposal

My reaction to Joe's engagement? Surprise. At the reception
following the graduation ceremony, I asked him, "What would
you have done if she had said no?" To be honest, I didn't think
it would last. He didn't seem to be himself that day. He was in a
different world on graduation day. It wasn't real.

—*my mom*

The last thing I wanted was for the show to damage my relationship with Nic. I know it may sound odd after all we'd been
through, but I profoundly wanted to be with Nic and that was the
only thing on my mind. I felt ready for the next stage in my life,
and that meant marriage. I alluded to this in my "confessional"
just before leaving to go home for my graduate-school graduation
ceremony. I hinted that graduating would be the start of a new
chapter in my life, maybe this, maybe that, maybe marriage. . . .

I initiated the purchase of the Tiffany's engagement ring in New
York City the day before my proposal/graduation. To figure out
her finger size, I had played with her fingers, massaged her hands,
and generally sized up what I had to. She had no idea what was on
my mind. Just two days before the ceremony, I went into Tiffany's,
immediately saw the ring I wanted, talked to the salesperson about
how quickly he could make the purchase happen with the credit
checks and ring sizing, and was out the door. It was a huge step and
I still wasn't completely sure—but I decided to go for it anyway.
Despite my doubts about our erratic relationship, later that day I
initiated the purchase. The next day, after the credit check came
through, I negotiated a finance plan for the ring with the promise
of being able to pick up the sized ring the next day, graduation day.

I orchestrated the day of graduation like a maestro. I attended a pre–graduation ceremony party with Nic and during the party, I knew I had to sneak out and pick up the ring without Nic knowing. Joe, the host, agreed to cover for me as long as he could. He didn't know what I was up to, but he was a good sport and played along.

Being held up at Tiffany's kept me away from the party longer than I had anticipated. Nic was bumming mad because I had left the party without any explanation. By the time I returned we had to leave for the ceremony.

Almost everything shot for the graduation episode is edited out of order. In some scenes, Nic is wearing her engagement ring before I even proposed. They show us in a horse-drawn carriage ride through Central Park together before I even pop the question, and the ring is already on her finger. That is certainly standing proof of the bogus sense of continuity on the show.

My parents didn't even know I was going to propose. I had no idea who was in the audience when I walked off the graduation dais, MBA diploma in one had, engagement ring hot in the other. I was in a daze—totally focused on Nic—walking in a cloud of nervous happiness. I dropped to one knee at Nic's feet, and whispered the words I had rehearsed over and over in my heart, and I made sure that the cameras couldn't hear me when I proposed. I wanted at least that to be private. When they were editing that episode, the director asked me if I would be willing to go into a sound booth to do a voice-over for them, so they could dub it to my lips moving and everyone could actually hear it. I said, "No way!" I'm pretty psyched that no one really knows what I said. It keeps the moment more personal.

But the moment certainly didn't go as smoothly as I had hoped. I kept the ring in the box and I wasn't sure if I should give it to her with the box wrapped, the box unwrapped, or with the ring in my hand from the start. So I just gave her the whole wrapped box. She didn't know what to do with it or what to say. The ceremony was quite loud, so she kept asking, "What did you say?" I kept saying, "Open it! Open it!" I ended up proposing about three times until Nic finally comprehended what was going on. She was really surprised, speechless actually. But she finally managed to call me a ham, and accept. We embraced for what seemed like an eternity.

Many people nearby were trying to figure out what was happening. All I knew was that it felt like the right time and place to make it happen. I wanted to be with Nic forever.

I made the commitment, publicly, to the right woman, on the perfect day. I was so happy. The proposal symbolized so many things for me. It became a positive gesture that would follow me forever. It could've followed *Nic and me* beautifully forever.

Family members, friends, and concerned fans of the show wanted to know why I combined huge events like my graduate-school graduation and a marriage proposal. They didn't want me to shadow the importance of my MBA degree. It was a big deal for me and for them. I took "my" day and made it a day for Nic and me. I thought that would be a special gesture of unselfishness on my part. I felt she deserved that for what we'd been through.

No one in my family had ever really had the opportunity to get to know Nic. My sister Christina had met her once, and maybe one or two others met her briefly at a quick dinner or something. The whole thing was a shock to everybody. My dad fell silent. I think he had a difficult time accepting the idea. He didn't say a word to me, from the moment I proposed through the entire graduation reception. His eyes became bloodshot, but he managed to stay until the end of the party for me—I really love him for that. Meanwhile, my mom was even cooler about it all. Right away she welcomed Nic to the family with open arms. Somehow this event brought the family closer together. This was supposed to be the best day ever in the life history of Joe Patane.

I found out that my dad actually did take the opportunity to speak with Nic at the reception. I couldn't believe it. She told me he said something like, "I'm happy I got a chance to talk to you, I know you better now." It was a brief talk, but his message seemed to be, "I feel more comfortable in the fact that you do love my son, and that you'll take care of him," something like that. His gesture deeply touched us.

Nic called her mom in the middle of the festivities to tell her the wild news. Her mom didn't believe it, but said she was happy for us. Both families had reservations about our marriage because neither parents really knew the person their child was marrying.

After the engagement, I made a reluctant return to Miami. Mike, however, staged a big surprise "Happy Birthday, Graduation, Engagement" party for me. It was exceptionally thoughtful of him and the others. Somehow, Mike managed to round up many people, including Saul, Landon, *Ocean Drive* staff, the roomies and more. The only person missing was Nic.

A few days after the party was when they sent us all to the Bahamas. I looked forward to this retreat to do some soul searching about all that had recently transpired. Of course, Nic was bothered by the prospect of me frolicking around some tropical island with my bikini-clad roommates. (As cute as Dan looks in a bikini, I told her not to worry.)

Once again, something happened to Nic as soon as I went back to Miami. All of a sudden, she wanted to send the ring back to me. Our whole relationship quickly became an off-and-on thing again. One minute she was enamored with me, but the next I was the bad guy.

As It Stands

I have come to believe that the primary source of evil lies in our ability to deny our own pain, fear, and vulnerability. In our mistaken belief that we can protect ourselves from life as it is, we inflict the worst horrors onto others and ourselves.
> —*Rosa Naparstek, June 1997, Fordham University atrium art display*

When the shows began to air a few weeks after we moved out of the house, Nic hit the roof. But not before she hit it off with other men in Italy: believe it or not, she took off to Italy to model the day after I finally returned from Miami. This time, instead of pushing me to Miami, she ran away to Italy. Meanwhile our whole relationship became a topic for friends and complete strangers to scrutinize. People wouldn't leave us alone, and a strong animosity grew between us. I'd call her often to work through our issues and the bitterness we felt toward each other. But by the end of most of the conversations, my contempt for her would have doubled, and hers for me would have tripled. I didn't know what was going on.

I thought I was jumping through more than the normal boyfriend-fiancé hoops to make Nic happy. But it wasn't enough for her. I didn't feel I was getting much of anything but contempt in return.

If I had come back from Miami having been completely faithful to Nic the entire time and found out about the other men, I would've felt like a fool. I'm sure the same holds true for her.

I learned something terribly disturbing through this experience. I always thought that if you cheated on somebody, it meant you were strong, because you were being sly by outsmarting the

other person. Now, I realize that cheating on someone means you're not being true to yourself. You have to be well rounded, with a good head on your shoulders, not to cheat. People who cheat are screwed up in the head. I'm just glad I realized it when I did, and not when I'm forty-six. It's an evolution of your soul . . . and if you don't learn it now, you'll come back to repeat it.
        —*Nic*

We were both playing the same silly games, trying to outdo one another. We both ended up losers in the end. When people, especially available women, began recognizing me in public, I started isolating myself, afraid that the old Joe would emerge. I really just wanted to be with Nic.

Nic helped me realize that I wasn't happy with being a lying, cheating, womanizing jerk of a guy. I can't imagine the pain it caused Nic to see my behavior on television. I once *heard* about Nic in a photograph with a guy and I couldn't even handle the *thought* of seeing it. Coming to terms with this made me begin to at least recognize her pain from hearing about or watching the show—and that pain began to stir up inside of *me*.

Over the phone from Italy, she told me numerous times that it was over. We talked and argued for hours and hours and hours on the phone. Sometimes I'd call her five times a day. She hardly ever called me, even though I'd sent her a calling card. I thought we were still engaged—I sent her faxes, gifts, flowers, and I even flew over on Independence Day to surprise her, but she told me to fly back. She still had the ring, but of course she hadn't brought it to Italy with her.

It seems like I've always been chasing Nic. I hope one day we can communicate and write together to help ourselves and others work successfully through the pain. She once wrote a poem that admitted that looking at me is like seeing herself. It was so beautiful and true for both of us. We messed up a potentially incredible thing.

> It's hard to know if being on *The Real World* is the only thing
> that spoiled my relationship with Joe. I mean, on the production
> side of the show, they don't make things happen, all they do is
> reveal. *The Real World* simply accelerated what would have
> inevitably occurred. That's why I'm so glad I didn't marry this
> guy and have all this happen behind my back without knowing
> about it. I thought of Joe in a really positive, good way before he
> went down to Miami. But that was the only side he revealed to
> me. I saw his true colors when he was on the show.
>   —*Nic*

One day, I "accidentally" bumped into Nic at the Port Authority Bus Terminal in New York City. She had left me a message earlier that morning saying she was going home to visit her family. She seemed to have been trying to reach out to me. I stood only five feet across from where she sat with her bags and stared right at her, but she didn't even notice me. I sat down and waited for about ten minutes, just observing her from a distance. She kept looking all around, nervous and worried, staring people up and down. I wanted to understand her and what she goes through every day.

She sat five feet in front of me and never looked in my direction. She turned her head in every other direction, worried about everything around her, looking up from her magazine. I kept thinking, Nic, just read the magazine instead of worrying so much about what's going on around you. You'd be so much better off. When she finally caught my eye, relief spread across her face and she came over to me. She held me and hugged me, and told me how happy she was to see me.

With old ladies and the bus driver looking at us, Nic and I continued our embrace, and she asked if I had purchased a ticket to join her. She looked in my pocket and saw that I indeed had a ticket. I told her I would go in a second but I didn't want to continue to be the source of problems in her family or upset her any further via the constant repetition of different episodes. She got on the bus alone and headed home while I waved to her from the platform.

I feel that Nic has a lot of things to get out of her system and resolve with her family, friends, work, and herself, just like I do, before she can handle a serious relationship. We've been hurt by people we loved or trusted, including ourselves, for a long time without getting the proper guidance.

Nic and I came to a crossroad last summer on what to do about our feelings for each other: we would either forgive each other for the pain we inflicted, or end our relationship without resolution. This is about the time I stumbled upon God and the rosary, a confused, frustrated soul looking for answers. I heard a talk by Dr. Paul Vitz at a Wall Street Catholics Young Adult Meeting about the need for forgiveness in relationships. He pointed out that forgiveness is central to our faith, and that the barrier to forgiveness is hatred. I learned that I can't always control my anger. Problems stem from holding on to the anger (which is normal and natural), but then cultivating it, almost enjoying it, and setting it in a kind of psychological cement that becomes hatred. When I really hate someone, and I was as close as it gets to hating Nic because of her not being with me, the person who was most hurt by that hatred was myself.

Until we can confront ourselves and our own need for forgiveness, recognizing our contributions to the problems in our own life, we aren't in a position to forgive other people. Forgiveness doesn't come easily, simply, or cleanly, but we find in it a profound capacity to bring healing: it's at the center of our faith. Once I came to realize that, I believed there was some kind of hope for Nic and me. We had plenty of work to do to fix our relationship, but at the center of my faith in our relationship, right next to trust, was forgiveness. I made an all-out attempt to get her back, but she wasn't at the same place.

I see why it's easy for people to get lost in the world of modeling, a beautiful world made up of facades and unrealities—a great place to cover up one's pain, both physically and emotionally. It seems the world is supposed to love a smiling model; it's a place where Nic can *bravely* hide her pain. I hurt for Nic. I really hurt for what I have done to her. I hurt for the pain the show has caused her. And I hurt for all the things in her and my life that are or were destructive. I write this book for therapeutic, constructive closure. I could make money and gain fame in much less painful ways if I really wanted to. Instead, I chose to self-analyze and renew myself. Nic thinks, at the time I write this, that I want the fame and I am guaranteed to be exploited again. I hope she is wrong.

It doesn't matter what Nic did to me when I was on the show. Her world, like mine, was shattered, but I hope that the destruction will allow for reconstruction—as it did for me. My message to Nic is simple: "Nic, wherever you are, whatever you do, I love you," I wrote when we spent some time in Central Park writing together. "You have confronted me with myself and I have awoken from my heartless slumber. Thank you!" It is true, if it's meant to be, for us to be a couple again, it's meant to be. Time will tell.

STARTING TO TEAR

How can I deny my love for you?
Your lips so sweet, my heart so new
I love, I care, I give my all
My darling sweetheart, hear my call
So alive are we
So shattered the rest
Many wonder why
I achieved the best . . . you
Give in to love
Creation so real
The Lord above
Has made it feel . . . true
Honesty, faith, respect, a dear heart
All ours in the shadows of lives once apart
But for now, I shout out, for all to adhere
Just leave Nic alone, she's starting to tear!

CHAPTER SIX

My World

When I saw Joe on that show, he really disappointed me. I thought, I really must have let him down as a father. The biggest goal I had for him was to get him through college, graduate with his master's degree, and become satisfied with a career—any career, whatever he wanted. I just wanted him to be happy. How much more can a father give to his son? What more could you want to give your son?

—*my father*

I'm sure there's a possibility that much of the following will be taken out of context, but at least I'll know the text is here for all who want to know the facts, instead of leaving the truth lying in a giant, dormant pile of film on *The Real World*'s cutting-room floor. It's embarrassing to even bring up some of these stories anymore, and I again apologize for any errors in memory or judgment.

The Long Trip Home (Disappointing Dad)

Shortly after the show began airing, I went home to visit the family. Immediately upon entering the house I detected a foreboding tension. I knew something was very wrong when my mother had trouble making eye contact with me.

My dad sat me down and said something like, "Okay, Joe, you were just on television, and I see you there, calling me names and saying bad things about me. That's something I have to deal with. But I'll give you a year—I'll support you for a year. Not in any financial way, but I'll give you whatever support you need. We'll remain father and son for another year." And that was that—end of our discussion. We didn't discuss his feelings about how I had hurt him, he didn't let me explain why I said what I said, or even let me apologize for offending him. Talking about feelings with my dad was never easy.

My father understands that they edited scenes for entertainment value—not Bob Hope–type entertainment, but today's crazy entertainment. He believes I got caught up in the Miami scene and the thrill of being on television. He had finally maintained some faith in me and my personal and business talent before I went on *The Real World,* but when he saw me on the show, he felt like everything between us was a bust. He was shocked to hear me claim on screen that my unhealthy attitudes toward women largely originated from his making statements like, "Joe, women are the downfall of men," when I was growing up. He never knew I harbored these feelings because we didn't talk about our emotions with each other. He thought I was more prudent. But I lost him and most of my discretion when I went on *The Real World*.

The next time I visited, I went having to ask my dad for something I vowed never to ask for—a monetary loan to help pay mounting credit-card debts. He unequivocally directed me out of the house, screaming, "You're not my son!" That's when I felt like everything had failed—my business, my relationship—and now the only people I thought I could count on were my parents, but my father refused to help me. My mom and my sister Christina were in the room when this happened. If my mom hadn't been sitting right there, I might have done something foolish—like actually leave.

Christina had experienced a similar issue with credit cards and said to me, "Look, *I'll* give you the money, but you have to promise to cut up your credit cards! You have a disease." I screamed, "Listen, I'm trying to get over this disease and I actually have a plan that nobody wants to listen to! Here Dad is, throwing me out of the house when I finally thought I was doing something right for a change. Now that's blowing up in my face, too!" I was furious and had little control over every bottled emotion that began pouring out.

Christina shouted back at me, "What, you think Dad is happy about what he saw on TV? It's killing him inside! It's killing him!" I asked my dad if this was true, I wanted to know how he felt. He looked me in the eyes and said, "You're killing me, son. I want you out of here."

His words stunned me and I slipped onto the couch. Blood rushed from my heart to my head, pounding and drowning out all sense of time. I never cared so much for anything more in my life than my relationship with my father and here we were fighting over money and my idiotic behavior on television. At that point, I felt completely empty, no family, no love, no money, no support. I broke down crying. All I really wanted was to make my father proud of me, show him how much I loved him and deserved his faith in me, but I had seriously failed.

As always, my mom, who sems to be the person who can make sense of anything, came to my rescue. I feel she is the strongest woman in the world—eight kids, just imagine that! She understands my dad so well, and loves him intensely. She knew that they had used footage out of context, and understood that they had put the program together with the aim of accenting the more entertaining and controversial parts.

I wrote her a letter after the incident with my father that expressed how much I appreciated her strength, how it inspired me, and how I loved her. I also wrote a letter to Christina that said, "While you were screaming at me at the top of your lungs, wanting to punch me out, you were still willing to write me a check for $18,000—I know this is a sign that you love me. This gesture and your care saved me from absolute devastation. Thank you for extending your love to me when I needed it most." My dad did eventually bail me out of this jam, but my sister's verbal support and generosity encouraged me to really conquer the "disease."

I'd had financial problems before, and still managed to pay for my tuition at Fordham with money I'd saved over the years. By my junior year, however, my frivolous spending on good times with my friends caught up with me, and my dad had to bail me out for a semester; I'd vowed that would never happen again. That's another reason he was so pissed at me: he saw me on *The Real World* claiming to have paid for college on my own. The truth is, I accepted a check from him during my junior year and he'd given me plenty of securites in my youth. I was brought up in a solid family environment that made me feel safe, secure, and loved. In fact, I actually paid for only 75 percent of college. It was wrong of me to take all the credit.

Disappointing Myself

There's a scene in *The Real World* where two girls are standing with me in a bar and I'm holding a beer. One of the reasons that scene hurts me so much is because of a serious car accident I'd had several years earlier on an icy street under the Brooklyn Bridge. When a police officer finally showed up, the first thing he asked was, "Were you drinking?" I made it clear to him that I wasn't a drinker and he wouldn't find a trace of alcohol in my system. But he assumed otherwise when he discovered beer in the back of my car. I'd forgotten that my buddies had left the beer there. I threw it over the pier, into the East River, yelling, "Screw that! That's not me!" I'm not a drinker and I don't even smoke. The only time I'd ever had a beer in my hand was when I wanted to fit into a social situation. I wouldn't drink it all—I'd milk one drink for the whole night. I realized firsthand how asinine it is to assume that holding or drinking beer is good for a person's image, because just having those beers in my car caused me more grief than I can ever explain.

That accident affirmed my desire to live. I couldn't move the next day when I awoke, but I was alive without major injury. (The only real injury I received came from the insurance companies.)

It's not my style to be drinking, and that's how I was seen in that episode. That scene infuriates me. If you look at the bottle, you can tell it's practically full and I was "image"-milking it the whole night and acting like "the man" with the ladies, just like in the bad old days. What an idiot I still was. I certainly had regressed.

Coming Home

When the *Real World* cameras followed me home to Brooklyn at Easter time, my mom took one look at the crew and said, "We want no part of this show. It's not the real world you're portraying. You can't possibly live in the *real* world without having a safe place to retreat from the world, or you'll go crazy." Unfortunately, she was only able to keep them away for one day.

The crew busted my family's chops trying to get into the house, but my parents refused. The crew had been sitting outside my parents' house in a van for a few hours before I arrived. I purposely missed my flight and took another so that I wouldn't have the crew traveling with me on my plane. I tried to pull this trick as often as possible. If I missed the plane, the crew never had enough time to track me down and rearrange their plans. This allowed me a couple hours of privacy before they caught up with me again.

Before I arrived, the crew kept knocking on my parents' door asking if they knew where I was and could they set up their equipment to do some filming in the house before I got there. My parents weren't going for it. They emphatically told them, "Absolutely not, no, uh-uh, go away, bub-bye."

When I finally showed up, the crew laid into me about my obligation to give them access to the house. Thank goodness my parents wouldn't give in to the pressure from the crew. They were totally cool. My mom said, "Joe, I want you to have a safe haven, to be able to come here whenever you need to. I want you to know that your house is a place where you can come when you need refuge." She knew I was going through a lot of pain.

It was the most wonderful feeling to know my family was protecting me from further exploitation. They could sense my exhaustion and need for seclusion. At the same time I had to listen to the people in the van complain, saying things like "Joe, you've got to let us in, it's your contractual obligation! You have to talk your family into letting us have access! In fact, they should have known this long ago! What's going on? You've gotta let us in! We want to get the whole story of your family, because it's very important to the show's storyline. We want to see the big Italian family side of your life. How else will the audience be able to understand your dad's effect on you, or the way you interact with your brothers and sisters? It's Easter! You can bring in aspects of your religion and your faith to boot! Come on, Joe, open the door."

For some members of the crew, getting juicy footage was a point of honor—and a possible step up in their careers, since the more their material was used, the more likely it was that they'd be picked to direct the episodes, I guess, and juicy footage seems to be what they showed the most. They'd say anything to coax their way into anywhere, but stronger people like my parents wouldn't budge.

They desperately tried to work every angle, but it wasn't working. Meanwhile, my sister Christina started feeling sorry for them because they were outside for so long. So she loaded up a mammoth plate of food and took it to the van. She asked, "Would you like anything to drink? You're going to be out here for a while, because we're not letting you in." It was so unbelievably funny that she did that. We all felt a little bad that these guys had to work on Easter and didn't get to celebrate. It was a good day for me, but a bad day for the crew.

Some episodes were surely a challenge to my personal and family life, but they say whatever doesn't kill you makes you stronger. "It opens lines of communication," co-executive producer Mary Ellis Bunim said to me. Yup, it sure did, and surprisingly, the show did effectively touch on life (both personal and business) and love, with many of the growing pains that come with them, and I think I'm better off for it.

There's a lot to say about my relationship with my father and how it's evolved through the whole *Real World* experience. My dad and I had it out after the show ended, but we hung in there together. We actually did communicate (you know, actually listening to each other instead of seeing who could yell the loudest). I used to leave my family in the dust when I needed to escape to my friends or a significant other, but the reality is that my family are the ones who will always be around, no matter what. You gotta appreciate 'em now, love 'em now, and enjoy it, not take it for granted. Pop is eighty now, and he's coming around nicely. I really do love him. We have a lot of catching up to do and I'm going to do my part to get there.

Discovery: Facing Myself

In high school, I was the kind of guy who just went home after school and spent time alone. My dad and mom insisted that I do my homework before going to play in Little League baseball or before I got to watch any television. Little League was basically my only heavy extracurricular activity, and lasted only one season, so when I discovered a local porno stash, my afternoons became much more eventful.

During these teen years, my dad retired, and he spent most of his time at home. We never really discussed relationships or sex. If a girl called the house, my dad would bellow, "What are you calling my son for?" I rarely went out on dates because he was so difficult about my interaction with girls. So I found solace in the porno stash. That was my way out, and that's how I learned about sex. I wanted to be like those guys in the videos, but I wanted to be nicer to the ladies than they were. I decided to make it my specialty. At an all-boys school, somebody had to be the expert, so I elected me.

As strict as my father was about limiting my interaction with the opposite sex, I wasn't lacking in that department. But the influence of pornography deeply affected the way I treated my female acquaintances. I turned every relationship into a game, not allowing myself to lose control emotionally or sexually with anyone. I've lost out because of this unhealthy attitude. Mentally, I'd brought pornography into my relationships to act it out with my girlfriends. It was an easy thing to get lost in. It ruined the relationships, and I degraded myself and my girlfriends in the process.

The Mirror Breaks

On more than one occasion, all the roommates got into telling each other stories about sexual conquests and experiences. Sure, it was immature, but that was the hottest topic in the house.

Cynthia would basically describe how she wasn't into experimenting sexually with her partners. Melissa, on the other hand, seemed to praise anything but ordinary situations when it came to sex. Melissa and I had lots of interesting conversations on the topic of sex, its nuances and deviations. In a way, however, talking to Melissa seemed *too* revealing.

On *The Real World,* I brought up the pornography topic to get a reaction from the other roommates—perhaps it was the beginning of my provocation for change, as Sue Dean would put it. Melissa had actually worked as a phone-sex operator and didn't seem to see anything wrong with the sex industry. She could justify everything she did, just like I used to, so we actually did get along in the beginning.

To me, Melissa seemed infatuated with porn magazines, videos, whatever. She appeared intrigued by them all, sort of like I was at the time. Seeing and hearing her, however, was probably what started turning me off to it all, because I saw an unattractive part of my personality through her, and it was nasty.

There were times when I *wanted* to be careful about what I said when the cameras were in my face, but wanted to find out more from others at the same time. This meant sharing more and more detail. Thank God I at least had the limited sense to hold back a little bit.

God couldn't even help me the one day when I mentioned how *I'd* actually aspired to be a porn star growing up. Ugh! I can't believe I did that! Now that it's out in the open, however, I can talk about it and get past it. I was as honest and open about sexual issues on camera as I could be given the circumstances, and explained the whole reason behind my interest in a porn career. But the full explanation never made it into the shows. So no one knows the whole story. Of course, I don't really want to be a porn star; it was simply my stupid, uninformed life goal *when I was an immature teenager.* That was what I wanted to do and I thought I would be the best at it. That's what defined manhood to me back then. What a shame! No adolescent should learn about sex through pornography, as I did—it gives a distorted view of reality and intimacy and is, generally speaking, just plain degrading to women. I grew up with warped views and have only recently made it above the battle.

I was excited about being on *The Real World* for the opportunity to bring up in conversation issues that affected young people, and I hoped I'd be able to set a good example. Well, that got messed up when the porn-star comment came up. It certainly pushed the wrong buttons, especially in my relationship with Nic.

After that episode aired, I got an offer from a big adult-video magazine to share an evening with any star, and all hell broke loose again. They wanted to take me out on the town with my favorite porn star, do a big interview, a photo shoot, the works. It was like a childhood dream, or more correctly, a child*ish* dream. I had my attorney call to see if it was for real, not to actually follow through on the offer, but to find out if they were for real and deny them if they were. I am so glad I chose not to do that interview. I'm having a hard enough time trying to heal the wounds inflicted on my family and friends from the show as it is. Being involved in something like that could have been considered a big macho thing when taken out of context, as it would probably be on *The Real World*. More correctly, it should be understood in context, pointing out my immaturity and disregard for myself and the people in my life by bringing the porn industry into our lives.

You'd think I'd have learned my lesson after the magazine called, but I pushed it one step further when I actually tried to make contact with a porn star who I was told had shown an interest in my character on the show. Thank goodness Nic was around to bust my chops and snap me back into reality. I never should have responded to either inquiry. I lessened myself and knew it wasn't right. I didn't want to be part of the porn scene. It was just intriguing to know the offer was there.

New Man

I'm sure this will sound strange in contrast to the preceding, but at another point in my life I seriously considered the priesthood. During the pornography years, I would have put becoming a priest on the same level with committing suicide. But I was looking for a way to make a profound difference in my confused world. I'm a strong believer in Christ working as a powerful force in people's lives. God's my buddy, and He always comes through for me, especially at times when I question my faith. I believe that a lack of faith, whatever the faith, brings you closer to death—and that faith brings you closer to life.

THE OLD DAYS

One of the many times I was traveling home to Brooklyn from working a summer internship for ITT in Stamford, Connecticut, I just let go of the wheel when my Volkswagen bug began to hydroplane in the nighttime rain. I thought, This is it. God, I'm totally in your hands. Please, don't let me hurt anybody. I didn't want to repeat my previous accident. Through the torrential downpour the car started spinning around and around for yards. I just wanted to get off the road, away from other vehicles. My car skidded backward in the mud off the side of the road for about another hundred yards, into a grove of trees, and then *Bam!* I slammed into a tree. Everything fell silent. I couldn't get out, and all I could see were tree limbs covering my windows. Suddenly, out of nowhere, I heard someone say, "Hey, dude, you all right?" I couldn't believe someone was out here in the pouring rain, in the middle of the night. He looked through my window and said, "Dude, I'm the guy you just hit! I was parked off the side of the road." It had happened again. But wouldn't you know it, I made it out relatively unscathed—*again*.

Both car crashes I've been involved in left me dumbfounded as to why I was still alive. I felt both invincible and helpless. When we realize that we ultimately don't have control of the universe and our time in it, we are ready to move forward with more fervor and the understanding that every day is a new and exciting day to be alive, to rebuild, to create, to love, and to grow.

THE NEW DAYS

During the second summer following *The Real World,* I decided to live and teach at St. Ignatius Summer Camp for kids in Crown Heights, Brooklyn. It was what my dream *Real World* living experience would have been—politeness, teamwork, learning, and sharing. I enjoyed the opportunity to give something back to the kids in my hometown, offering them hope for a better future. It also gave me much-needed time to reevaluate what I wanted to do with my life. Most of the camp staff, including me, lived in the parish rectory and participated in group prayer and common dinner and other household activities together on a daily basis.

At the time, Nic and I weren't getting along at all; my family was still upset with me about things I said and did on the show; my finances were shot, since getting a real job after being on *The Real World* seemed to be just walking into more pain; and practically no one—not even some old friends—believed or understood the changes I was going through. My only solace seemed to come from God. I wondered if maybe I should increase my role within the church to full-time.

I met up with an old college acquaintance, Joe Squillace, at the summer camp. He had been pursuing the Jesuit priesthood for three years. His parents had brought him up in a traditional Italian household like mine and wanted him to be a lawyer, but after a year of heeding his parents' wishes, he joined the Jesuits anyway. He's a year younger than me, and though I didn't know him well in college, I remembered his desire to serve others, and also his immature perspective on women that was similar to my own, until something happened suddenly and he decided to join the priesthood. This bizarre reconnection with Joe was the beginning of my final processing of that same plan.

While he studied in the priesthood, he met a woman and they gradually fell in love. As his feelings for her intensified, he assessed his reasons for joining the priesthood in the first place—was it really a calling, was it to get away from his parents, or what? He loved the reverent life but realized he didn't have to be a priest to live it and could still make a difference from the outside. Once he became completely honest with himself, he knew he had to leave—a tough decision, indeed.

Joe and I began to openly discuss our respective dilemmas. After a long day of teaching, community prayer, and dinner, we'd take walks together and talk about life. We reminisced about the stupidity of our particular relationships of the past and how far we'd come. We really came clean with each other. It wasn't like hangin' with the boys and talking trash; instead we shared something akin to confession sessions and spiritual direction. I wished I could erase the old phases of my life and thought joining the priesthood might be one way to absolve my past. I felt safe in the church and enjoyed caring and sharing, especially when working with the children, and in return I was treated with compassion, trust, and respect for who I really was. The realization came to me, however, that I was trying to avoid trouble with women by hiding in the church. I'd been feeling that if I couldn't be with Nic, I might as well take my vows.

While that summer snapped me out of any intention I had to join the priesthood, more importantly it rebuilt my self-respect and self-worth. After plenty of soul-searching, praying, and conversations with Joe, I left camp knowing I didn't want or need to go the extreme route. I had to find a different way to get through the pain of my relationship with Nic and with *The Real World.* Over that summer, I recognized that I could break old patterns by facing them head-on—not by running away. I didn't need to join the priesthood to prove to everyone that I have self-control and no longer want or need to be surrounded by lots of women. People can make their own assumptions, but the sordid past remains just that . . . the past. The camp experience reinforced my belief that I have a lot to offer—without entering the priesthood. I can share my outlook on life through many different venues. I can take advantage of the few positive aspects of the show and demonstrate my love of God, my new respect for women, and my optimism for the future without having to join the church.

Love and the Single Guy

Melissa made one comment on air that is difficult to live down. In one of her interviews, Melissa said, "I think Joe could be married, with five hundred children and he'll still be a womanizer." That line created so much adversity between Nic and me. It's amazing how much damage words can do.

I also got plenty of flak for a scene where a waitress in a restaurant flirts with me. I mean, come on, the cameras are on us, I'm being my normal, friendly self, and obviously she was into being on TV. In all honesty, back then if I hadn't been trying to be Mr. Loyal-to-Nic Guy, I would have tried to get to know an attractive waitress a little better, and used the cameras as bait like everybody did. I'm sure I was even trying to show off a bit for the roommates.

I believed this waitress was interested in me as soon as she saw me. As Melissa noted, I'd want everybody to know that women were falling for me, especially at a time when I was having problems with Nic, who wasn't with me much then and certainly wasn't being supportive. Consequently, I needed a little harmless attention.

In Miami, I kept thinking to myself, Nic, why can't you be nice to me, like that waitress was? All I need is to know that I've still got someone, because right now, Nic, you're not making me feel like I have anyone. I know it's an immature way to act, but the only person I loved and wanted to be with wasn't returning my affection. Nic put it plainly on the infamous two-on-one treadmill scene: "If I'm not here for you to bitch and complain to, you're gonna find someone else."

Mike got pissed off because I got a lot of attention from the girls in Miami. He figured it all has to do with my Brooklyn accent. Some buddies think it has more to do with my being relaxed, yet confident with myself. Who knows? Melissa reduced the whole incident to my loving to boast about the attention and wanting to make sure everybody knew what happened. Sure, it's silly, but they were just as fascinated as I was about why women were attracted to me. Now I don't even care very much.

I'm okay with being alone now, after coming to an acceptance of how being on *The Real World* has drastically affected me, my family, and my relationship with Nic. I enjoy my own company, and I don't need to be entertained by the attention of others. For the first time I'm realizing that I'm okay on my own; I don't need a lover to take care of me. I just want to love—love myself, love God. I want to have a *healthy* relationship with myself and my family. It's not scary to me anymore. This is a big breakthrough for the average jerky boy from Brooklyn.

CHAPTER SEVEN

Was It Real?

You've been chosen because those who've met you feel you have something interesting to share and that you will be a compelling addition to the group's dynamic.

—*Cast Welcome Pack*

We admit that—it's a television show. It's not a pristine social experiment. First and foremost, it has to be entertaining for its audience.

—*co-executive producer Jonathan Murray*

Bloopers

*D*ude! Watch your head!" But it was usually too late to save the camera guy from ramming into a tree. That was one thing that happened constantly on the *Real World* set—either blindered camera people crashed into doorways, or we'd suddenly turn around and knock a camera guy over. At other times, the guy holding a boom microphone would accidentally smack us in the head with the boom. Cameras and cameramen were the main problem, though. If we weren't tripping over them, they'd be knocking into lampposts or tripping over curbs themselves.

Certain of the crew had the esteemed pleasure of being on call to capture our every schizophrenic movement twenty-four hours a day. That meant having to live almost on top of us. Instead of making them sleep under our beds, some of the crew stayed in a house across the street from ours. I don't know if they slept there, but it seemed like a home base. They fenced it off and everything. We saw crew cars parked there all the time. It felt like we were living in a house being staked out by a spy ring.

Sometimes I actually felt sorry for the crew. They had challenging jobs, chasing us around, trying to get every important moment on film. If only you could have seen the sweat pouring off the cameraman when I bought the engagement ring for Nic at Tiffany's! They also had the pleasure of spending hours watching us like hawks when all we did was sit around the house, reading alone or working on the computer. I'm sure they had to put their own lives on hold while chasing us around for hours on end.

Invasion

There were times during our weekly personal interviews with the directors when they would ask questions I refused to answer. Some things seemed too personal to divulge, even for *The Real World*. That's when they'd get really pushy and "remind" me of my ridiculous contract. Sometimes I'd make something up just to give them an answer. Out of desperation, I'd say anything to make them happy and get them off my back. They must've learned their interview techniques from war interrogation-training films. As Flora put it, "We were totally manipulated. They cut you off in midsentence. They show things out of sequence. The director would sit there and ask us the same question twenty million times until we answered the way he wanted. The whole show was manipulated for us to fight."

Melissa constantly communicated with certain camera and sound people behind the scenes, both on-line and in person, even though it was against the rules for both sides. But she wasn't the only one; she was just the one who did it most often. All of the girls liked certain guys in the crew, fooling with them like it was a game, trying to get the crew to talk, or laugh, or whatever. Once in awhile the girls would unite and gang up on a crew guy just for the fun of it, joking into the camera lens and saying things like, "Hey, I wonder what you're all about—why don't you open your mouth? Talk to me. Let's get to know each other better." They were totally teasing the crew a lot of the time. Sometimes they went a lot further, brushing up behind the crew, grabbing them and things like that. Flora, as you may know from seeing the show, had a habit of flashing her breasts—taking it yet another step further.

There were definitely people in the crew I would've preferred hanging out with instead of my roommates. We had nicknames for every crew member. One guy we called Lucky Charms (because he looked like the cereal-box character). He dated Rachel from the San Francisco cast of *The Real World*. He and Rachel were in a car accident during the Miami filming and he didn't make it out alive. That was quite a blow to our crew, as evidenced by their faces after they heard about it. We cast members were generally left in the dark about it, however, and we weren't even "allowed" to attend the funeral services.

Occasionally, the crew would take our food, but only if we offered it. Whenever I barbecued, I always offered the leftovers to the crew. I mean, they had to be hungry, too, you know? Sometimes they were so worn out from chasing us around, I felt *obligated* to feed them. Once, a crew member actually cooked for us. He happened to be a gourmet chef and wanted to prepare everything we caught from a day of deep-sea fishing. The problem was, if the directors or producers found out that the crew interacted with anyone from the cast, they'd get their heads handed to them—and several were fired for this reason.

Being a *Real World* crew member was definitely a dangerous job. They should've hired stunt people. Flora actually ran over the foot of one crew member while she was trying to make a fast getaway in her car. I wonder if she really messed up his foot. Melissa was another madwoman at the wheel of her car when she was trying to outrun the cameras. Most of us tried to speed away from the crew, but they would still try to block the cars.

At one point, I became so disillusioned with being on the show that I decided to make my own getaway. I grabbed my bags, ran to my rental car, and tried to drive off, but a production member halted me by leaping in front of the car and saying something like, "You can't go anywhere! Everyone needs you!" He stood in front while other crew members blocked the back of my car and, of course, kept the film rolling. I told him he was making me late and to get out of the way. He wouldn't budge. He told me to wait for the director, who was summoned to chat with me. Upon the director's arrival, I was assaulted with a barrage of baloney again. "You're a hero, you're a champion! What you're doing is incredible! You have such a beautiful story to tell! You have to tell the story of your family, your love, and your difficulties! You should be sharing it with the world! It's something everybody goes through!" Blah blah blah. He actually made me believe him. The director finally did let me leave for the weekend, on the condition that I would return on Monday with a full Confessional-booth report. I agreed, only after he promised I could have that whole weekend *without* the cameras. And so it was ... my one-time escape from the Alcatraz house. I cannot tell you how amazing the feeling was when I drove off into the sunset with Nic by my side, and no prison walls or surveillance to be had for the many-mile drive to our final destinations of Key Largo and Key West.

The Confessional was another technical nightmare. Half the time, we'd forget to turn the camera on and talk for fifteen minutes before realizing it. We'd have to start all over, repeating the whole thing. Other times the camera wouldn't work, I'd forget to put a tape in the camera, the lightbulbs would burn out, the backdrop would fall down, or Leroy the dog would bark constantly—it was classic TV blooper time.

One incident occurred during the season that was in complete breach of talent–crew interaction. It happened the weekend I planned to propose to Nic. A crew member was hungry for some romantic footage of Nic and me together. In a desperate attempt to create the right mood, he pulled me aside, gave me a couple of bucks, and told me to enjoy that horse-drawn carriage ride around Central Park with Nic.

It felt strange taking a carriage ride at that time and under those circumstances. When you live in New York City, it feels awkward to do tourist-type things like that in the first place. Plus, a carriage ride seemed a bit too hammy in union with my marriage proposal, already deemed "hammy" by Nic. Nonetheless, we agreed to go along with it, because it seemed so important to the crew. At first I thought, Wow, they're doing this to be nice. But I knew better: it was all for the camera and the nice, *romantic* storyline, so I was game. At least it was a nice gesture, insofar as it turned out cute and romantic—unlike other offers that, not surprisingly, turned on us in the final cut. There are certainly worse things they could have staged (and probably did, without our knowing it).

As I mentioned earlier, they made it appear as if Nic and I took the carriage ride before I proposed to her, but if you look closely, you can see the engagement ring on her finger. That's an example of how they present events out of order. This sort of thing turns up constantly in the episodes. Sometimes, I'll see myself wearing four different shirts on one show—in one evening! More often than not, they've edited the events of several different evenings into one. Believe me, my wardrobe isn't large enough to change shirts four times in one night. Something fishy was obviously up in the fishbowl for you all to recognize on screen, if you cared to. Sorry, but it's true.

In/Sanity

I thought we were all headed for the psycho ward when the show ended. That's the reality, whether other cast members want to admit it or not. I can only compare it to what it must be like being in a cell block (granted, a high-style one), or just plain being caged for five and a half months. It takes time to decompress from the show and having cameras in your face 24-7. Bottom line, we came out a complete mess! It's not as if there was a therapist for us to call and talk to about the emotional strain the show puts on us. We were left to cope on our own, not sure of where to go or who to turn to for help, for fear of breaking one of the rules or terms of the contract.

There was only one time when I thought a director was conducting an inventory of our emotional well-being, but it turned out that it wasn't for use on the show. Several weeks into the show, he interviewed each of us with a personal video camera. Maybe he was doing some kind of psychological profile. Who knows? It was the only time he asked questions about how we were doing, how we felt, what it was like to have cameras around us all the time. The whole tone of the interview was unlike the usual routine. It was really refreshing to be asked how I felt instead of dishing out personal dirt for them to turn into entertainment. They should've done that more often just to make us feel better.

One night, in a cab ride home from taping a commercial for the show with Kevin Powell from the New York cast, Mary-Ellis Bunim, one of the show's executive producers, asked if I thought anything should be included in the contract for future cast members. I mentioned the potential need for therapy. Maybe she thought I was kidding, but I wasn't. It's probably the reason the commercial never aired.

Unfortunately, even during the candid psychological interviews, some cast members appeared to still be "acting" for the camera. They weren't able to profoundly dig deep inside themselves to separate who they were on camera from real life and real emotions. Or maybe that was their technique to safeguard their sanity. In this environment, there will always be people who try to manipulate the medium by masking their true personalities from the camera as well as people who honestly try to be themselves. Most likely, everyone falls somewhere in between—there's no way anyone could fully be themselves given the extraordinary circumstances.

My buddy Mike witnessed the "poser factor" firsthand when he came to visit during the last month of filming. Mike dislikes Florida, and strongly opposed the South Beach mentality. He could detect the phoniness a mile away. He didn't have a problem feeling comfortable in front of the cameras because he works in the entertainment business and it's part of his job. The whole *Real World* environment hit him as being *completely* artificial. He feels it wasn't the cameras that created this synthetic world, it was the way people acted in front of them. He saw the obvious attempts that some cast members made to articulate a clever sound bite just because the camera was sitting there. He noted the crew's subtle, encouraging responses when a person said or did something worthy of making it into the show. Some of the roommates ate this up and sound-bited away, just to get air time. A combination of all these factors truly diminished the show's reality-based flavor.

Flora and Melissa put on a good show when we all got the word to go to the Bahamas. Melissa stressed how she had to attend her brother's graduation and couldn't go. And somehow Flora managed to use a similar story. If you watch the episode closely, you can see that they do a lousy job of excuse making.

Allegedly, a crew member had clued Melissa and Flora into the nature of the trip when he informed them that we would be camping in tents on a secluded island with no indoor plumbing or outlets. This did not excite the ladies and was probably the reason that they got out of going. That completely altered the outcome of the events of that experience. It would've been an entirely different camping trip had Flora and Melissa been with us. It once again compromised the so-called integrity of the show.

Opportunity Nots

From a business perspective, there are a million commercial opportunities for the average *Real World* cast member to pursue, yet few take advantage of that potential. So many decent people who have been on the program ended up being indecently exploited by a network that can do whatever it wants to with our images. It's as if our personalities and likenesses are possessed by a cable network and are no longer our own. I think it would be great to see more cast members reclaim their identities and turn the tables around to repackage and even resell themselves in a way that gives them their true or new identity back. Our "characters" will be with us forever. We're trapped inside that show, stuck in repeats for eternity, like *Gilligan's Island* castaways, but actual living and breathing "real" castaways, not just characters representing them.

Many opportunities have come and gone for me and others since being on the show. For instance, after I bought the engagement ring, Tiffany's was interested in my creative marketing concept to do a series of commercials with Nic and me. Unfortunately, they were currently in production with another television commercial and had already established their marketing campaign for the upcoming year, so that one never came to fruition. Another lost opportunity was when I was contacted by the president of a company that sells a skin-healing cream. He'd seen the show and noticed the scar on my neck; he thought I would be a good business partner and spokesperson for the product, but that didn't play out either.

Freebies and Perks

Mike had a genius scam going when he worked for *Ocean Drive* magazine. One of his techniques for selling ad space was to have the cameras go with him on calls. A certain percentage of businesses realized that they could possibly gain free exposure if Mike frequented their establishments with the camera crew in tow. Amazing how well this motivated his clientele and lined Mike's pockets with commissions.

Not every client made the cut, but a few got into episodes, mainly the restaurants. Mike loved to finagle freebies out of places, especially free meals or tee times at a local golf course. Some members of the cast did almost everything for free, from parasailing to nightclubbing. In fact, it was one of Mike's deals that landed us that deep-sea fishing trip. They never showed that excursion on the show, but viewers can see Mike and me eating up our catch that the rule-breaking crew member had cooked for us.

One of the coolest hookups I landed was a trip to a Lazer Tag camp in Coconut Grove. I actually got all seven roommates to go, and had a bunch of my buddies from home join in as well. That was one of the few times we had done something as a group, but the cameras didn't follow. It's a shame that they weren't there, because it was a rare occasion where we got along and enjoyed each other's company—perhaps it was because the cameras *weren't* there. I guess the cameras didn't come inside because the darkness and the lasers may have caused lighting difficulties. I'm sure the crew appreciated the brief time off from having to chase us around. We sure appreciated the break, no matter how short, from them. We all went to the Cheesecake Factory afterward and pigged out. The crew was there, since they'd been waiting outside the Lazer Tag place to follow us when we finished.

The cast got to keep little things from the house when the show wrapped. They would never have parted with major things like the bikes or the Wave Runners, but we walked out of there with Rollerblades, knapsacks, flip-flops, suntan lotions, T-shirts, and that sort of thing. Once in a while we would score stuff from area businesses, like soda from a local soft-drink manufacturer or free food from a local restaurant. My personal favorites were the Snoopy merchandise hookups. That was awesome.

Reality

It's difficult to imagine a multimillion-dollar house filled with seven post-teenage strangers thrown together to start a business for themselves while cameras stare on, as *reality*. But it *was* an opportunity like no other. I guess it's as close as a television show can get to "reality-based" programming without being an actual documentary. It's more like a docudrama/soap opera. Unfortunately, *real people* are the ones who end up looking foolish, thanks to the creative editing used to spice up the show for optimal viewing pleasure.

When I was going through the interview process, I was excited about everything I was learning about myself. No one had ever really asked me questions like they were asking, and it made me think about my position on a variety of topics. They presented an incredibly idealistic situation for someone looking for an entrepreneurial challenge. However, they failed to point out that the "reality" of the stories they presented on the show is based on real lives, cut and edited into entertaining pieces, but does not necessarily document these lives explicitly or accurately, as that would take years of air time. What a nice flaming loophole. Unfortunately, I jumped right through it.

Most of what I ended up seeing on television is not what I remember happening. I mean, they take sound bites from months after a video clip and patch them together. That confused everything. It made me feel all messed up inside to watch. On some level, I imagine every cast member who's been on *The Real World* feels similarly messed up from this experience. I remember Jonathan Murray saying something like, "Joe, it's not real, it's your lives, yeah, but it's made for television. You've gotta *laugh* about it." But you know what? It's not funny.

Throwing yourself at the mercy of the cameras has its advantages, if you're strong enough to handle it. I definitely got a good look at my dark side. I have issues to resolve, and being on *The Real World* brought many of them to the forefront, forcing me to deal with them straight up. To face your shortcomings alone is difficult. To have them shoved in your face on international television is quite disturbing, yet, interestingly enough, quite therapeutic if you're willing to go the distance like I have. I hope all the past cast members and people affected by the show can do the same. I learned who I want to be, what kinds of people I want to live and work with, what my limitations and strengths are, and the advantage of being "de-masked" to the world. It's a whole new life.

Too Far

The cameras followed us into most public places, but I was especially upset when they followed me to church. One of the episodes shows me sitting near the aisle in one of the pews. Halfway through that service, I noticed a camera guy in the aisle, on his knees, filming me, and a sound guy who had positioned himself in the middle of the congregation, with the large boom in hand and a smile on his face. After the mass had begun, they even posted these huge release signs on the facade of the building stating that the area was going to be filmed, and by entering the building you gave permission to be on television, unless you objected. It was the same situation when I graduated in St. Paul's

Catholic Church, across from Fordham in New York City. But that was a more public event where any news crew could attend. This all seemed so wrong, distracting and disrespectful to everyone in the church and God. Then I thought, Maybe it is somewhat beneficial because it may be on TV and carry a positive message. After the show aired, I got E-mail from many people who really appreciated me for not being afraid to show my religious beliefs and be in church.

A main time I got really frustrated with the camera people was when I went to buy Nic's engagement ring at Tiffany's. The crew was freaking out. Richard, the camera guy, was like, "Joe, tell us what's going on. What are you going to do? What's happening? Are you buying a ring?" They followed me to Tiffany's but couldn't get permission to film in the store. They really had tough jobs trying to catch every important moment. They tried hard to get footage of the ring, but a Tiffany's security guard closely followed them throughout the store. I imagine Richard kept filming anyway, holding the camera by his side, claiming it was turned off. Richard was good. I'm sure he did get bits and pieces of the moment on film—or at least on the mike—but it never made it to air, apparently because Tiffany's doesn't allow filming in the store.

My attitude at that exciting time was, "You guys follow me all the time, anyway! Catch whatever you can. I'm going about my business like you're not even here, the way I'm supposed to—so just *try* to keep up."

That camera and sound equipment gets pretty damn heavy for the crew, especially when they're chasing someone down the street. I sprinted from that pre-graduation party to Tiffany's and back, and, like I mentioned earlier, I've never seen a cameraman sweat so much. It looked like he'd jumped into a pool—his entire being was soaked. I didn't give them trouble trying to film me, but

I didn't go out of my way to help them either. I'm sure they prayed I would take a cab—they probably would've paid for it at that point.

The crew knew that this day was a big moment in my life, probably the "climax storyline" of the season for my character and notably because, as Mary-Ellis Bunim is quoted as saying, it was *The Real World*'s "first on-camera proposal." Richard gave me grief: "Joe, this is going to be a big moment, and you're not helping us at all. Please, Joe, please, you gotta tell us, what's gonna happen?" But I wanted everyone to be surprised. I wasn't taking any chances that Nic would find out about the proposal before I asked. I offered Richard some reassurance by saying, "Look, like I said already, you're following me all the time, right? You're coming to graduation, right? You're filming everything, right?" Richard thanked me for that, trusting I was being straight with him. At that point, we knew each other quite well, because he was the guy usually assigned to follow me every day.

I hated Richard at times, and cursed him out, especially when he tried to go beyond the surface of my life and invade my psychological well-being. It was one thing to share, but it was another to let the experience drive me crazy.

Richard disclaimed his actions with something like, "Hey, it's my job, Joe, it's my job. It's in your contract, you're supposed to give it up to the camera. You have to give up your relationship, your family, your private life." I'm like, "Dude, you've ravaged everything of mine. My relationship, my family . . . you're killing me." He never backed off. We were on complete opposite sides of the fence.

From the time I insinuated that Richard would have a good angle on the day's extraordinary events, he began to trust me more. He realized that I would include him on all my most important moments if he gave me more space and time once in awhile. He was finally comprehending that I was a human being. He sincerely thanked me at my graduation, completely altering our relationship. He understood the pain I withstood, and the enormity of my decision to propose to Nic. Richard was very serious about the documentary process and would do anything to get the material. He was known for his tough tactics and no one really appreciated him. I did—but only after we'd reached this understanding.

Richard and I hugged at the wrap party. It was almost like a brotherly love we felt for each other, like army buddies who had gone through hell together. We had developed a mutual respect for each other.

When all was said and done, I generally expressed to the crew, "Thank God it's over! I'm sorry I busted your chops so many times, but you never stopped busting mine!"

See Ya!

The humiliation really kicked in at the wrap party when we were allowed to see the back control room and speak openly with the crew for the first time and found out just how invasive the *Real World* cameras were. They caught so many private moments of us, it felt violating. You never know what other people can or can't see through the lens, zoom and all. They don't make that clear enough in the Welcome Pack.

It was a disturbing experience when we checked out the control room for the first time. It was like facing this *thing* that had been controlling our lives. I thought it would be exciting to see where everything happened, until I saw all of the video monitors and video decks. I felt totally distressed. For some reason, the whole nature of the past five and a half months swept over me. I thought, Whoa, that camera can film *everything*—even when I didn't know it was there. Wow, they caught me there, and there—hey, where's that sound coming from? I went from the extreme happiness of ending the season to a queasy, sick feeling in my stomach.

Being able to talk to the crew for the first time was really weird. They approached us as if we had been buddies all along. I mean, I have to admit, there were times I grew to hate some of the crew members for their pushy insistence. But they all came up, slapped me on the back, laughing, saying, "Heyaah, Joe! We finally get to talk!" They felt like they knew me.

Imagine there are these people you don't even know, who have listened in on every detail of your life—not just relationship issues, but intimate details like your financial status, how much you make, how much you owe, the health of your great-aunt Erma in Iowa. It's disturbing. I thought, Who are you people? They were too eager to explain, analyze, and advise me on everything in my personal life, saying things like, "I wanted to say this to you when that happened, and I think it was cool what you did at your graduation, blah blah blah, I know you really love Nic and don't worry, she'll come around. . . ." It's like entering the Twilight Zone, and I was freaking. I didn't feel right when the crew approached me so informally, and I don't think they understood that.

It seemed the whole cast had a similar reaction. In an attempt to cheer us up, the crew let us play with the cameras. Being a technical nerd, I wanted to learn what went into producing the show, asking them to show me everything from sound processing down to the editing bay. They'd built an entire room for monitoring the twenty-four-hour surveillance cameras. It was hard to fathom that a mere wall separated us from all this equipment.

On the last day, *The Real World* donated most of our furniture to a nonprofit neighborhood youth program. A big semi truck pulled up, bundled the household furniture, put it on the truck, and hauled it off. Some of the cast members helped out, others didn't. In addition, we had a whole press day of interviews that just added to our overwhelmed feelings.

Final Word

I lived my life for five and a half months in a multimillion-dollar house with free rent and all the amenities. After the cutting and pasting, and doing everything they do to make their selected storylines work, including manipulating characters and sound bites to fit these storylines, it's hard to recognize ourselves as "real" individuals. The show is whatever they want to portray about our generation. I wanted to believe that they would show the diversity and uniqueness of members of our generation and how we can all reach a common ground. It seems as if they were looking to show our demise instead, because that seems to be what the public wants to see on television.

I don't believe that our generation is so extremely lost or needs a label. That's why I went on the show—to prove we can use our youthful energies positively—to power a company, work as a team, make a difference in the boardroom, whatever. We have ideas, dreams, and aspirations to do more than just "slack." I wish that the viewers had known more about our *real* lives, because the portrayals on the show don't represent the enormous potential that we all have to make a difference in the world. I believe anyone can do whatever they really believe in—that's the message I really wanted to send in the five and half months I spent on *The*

Real World: Believe in yourself, take risks, don't be timid about working hard—just harness the inspiration, and go for it.

As a result of the whole experience and the circumstances and processes revolving around the writing of this book, I feel that I have become a stronger, more mature individual, both personally and professionally. More than learning who I was, I began to figure out who I really want to be. I can now move forward to discover who that is, and become better.

CHAPTER EIGHT

Afterlife

I just want to shut my eyes and not see the place I've
been.
— *Brad Pitt,* Sleepers

So many people ask me, "How do you deal with having
been on *The Real World*?" Well, I ask myself that same
question. I once saw Sylvester Stallone in the street and knew he
was staying at a nearby hotel. I watched him for a while, getting
mobbed by people, but being a complete gentlemen to total
strangers. I wrote him a note that read, "How the heck do *you*
deal with that stuff?" (I'm still waiting for a reply.) I don't know if
there is a way to deal with being on *The Real World*. I've just
learned how to accept that I sacrificed my personal freedom and
privacy and I've gotta move on from it.

When the show aired, a lot of people started to recognize me. It
was hard enough when a camera followed me around, but now I had
total strangers doing the same thing. At first, it was flattering, then it
got scary. Most people I meet on the streets are really cool. They just

wave or smile or say, "Hey, what's up? Aren't you that guy from *The Real World*? That's cool! Take it easy." Others are only interested in the fantasy that *The Real World* created. They think it's their job to give advice about my personal life, referring to events that took place over two years ago as if they had just happened yesterday.

They ask, "How'd you deal with Flora? How's the business going? I can't believe you guys blew $50,000! What's up with Nic? You married yet?"—treating me like a familiar friend. They ask questions that take me back to a different time. They draw conclusions about *me* based on what they saw on *The Real World.*

Since the show ended, I've basically adopted a hermit's lifestyle. Going out during the day is like walking onto a mine-field; someone's always recognizing me. Many times when people walk past me, I can hear them giggle and chatter. If I happen to glance or turn around, they may be pointing at me or something silly like that. It's so weird when you don't know what people think of you. Some people feel compelled to touch me. Girls offer to sleep with me. Everyone seems to want a piece of me, or *The Real World,* or some form of television life for themselves. Sometimes I just wanna be plain old Joe again, when I didn't feel like a sightseeing attraction. Not a day goes by when someone doesn't come up to me and ask about the show. It locks the events of your life into some kind of television vacuum. It vacuum-sealed approximately 1 percent of 1 percent of my life that will forever define me in the world of television.

I've had to adapt to putting a new twist on normal activities just to avoid good or bad confrontations with strangers. For instance, I love to Rollerblade, but avoid going out during the day. So I blade through the streets of New York City at night. I enjoy it, actually, having the streets and the city to myself, skating under a blanket of solitude. I especially used to enjoy doing this with Nic.

So, how did I come to terms with the way my image is locked into the television world forever? Well, I know that the person on *The Real World* resembles me and who I was, but it's not who I am today. There's nothing I can do to change people's perception of me except through my everyday actions, now and into the future. Viewers saw only seconds of my life all garbled together during a limited period of time.

It's not as if any member of *The Real World* is currently playing a major role in a film and can escape behind another character. We're all trapped with our *Real World* image for the rest of our lives. It's like getting to the pearly gates of heaven, St. Peter rolls the film of your life, and production has already edited it for maximum entertainment value, complete with a soundtrack. I mean, they didn't exactly use the most flattering footage of us.

Immediately after the show ended, I spiraled downward into myself, closing everyone out, becoming tremendously self-involved and living in isolation. I lost my faith and trust in people—my innocence, in a way. I felt I had been dishonored, misrepresented, or just plain misled, and if *I* felt that way, I can imagine how the people close to me, especially Nic, must have felt. I lost the zeal I had for life. I lost the love and the faith. I didn't like what I saw on television. I didn't like who I was, let alone who they made me out to be—and all in all, I didn't know who I was anymore. Things were changing; something was happening inside me. I didn't want to let anyone in, and when and if I did, it was never without severe constraints.

Once *The Real World* replaces you with an android of yourself, there's no going back.
> —*Norm Korpi, of* The Real World's
> *New York City cast,*
> *in* Time Out New York, *July 10–17, 1996*

When I was picked to be a member of the *Real World* cast, I thought it would be an entertaining documentary highlighting me as a self-motivated entrepreneur of the twenty-something generation. But when I saw the first few episodes, I felt beaten. I felt reduced to a stereotype—Joe, the womanizing business guy. Although I ran my own business and had a lot of other things going on in my life, I felt reduced to a one-dimensional character.

One source of inspiration to dig myself out of my emotional grave came with an offer to join other members of past casts and tour the country, talking to college students about our experiences on the show. The best part of these talks is the opportunity to discuss things that matter, things that students have a difficult time dealing with, like being away from home for the first time, getting along with roommates, diversity issues, orientation issues, conflict resolution, relationships, and more. It's rewarding to have an audience of peers show up to hear me speak, but even more special is that they actually listen to my words and look to me as a role model. What I project to them today is posi-

> You know, sometimes in life, we often take flack from others—they try and tell us how to live, dress, or even whom we should date. It takes a strong, or maybe just an honest person to be like, "You know what? I will listen to your opinion and respect it, however it won't change me, my feelings, or my life decisions."
>
> —*fan E-mail*

tiveness and believing in yourself and doing the right thing—perhaps not what they would have expected from my "character" on the show.

As a person who has obviously been negatively affected by his past adolescent behavior, it's nice to know some students really take my words to heart. We all have growing pains, but have to find ourselves eventually and move on—the sooner the better. All the positive feedback I've received has encouraged me to believe that maybe there was a higher purpose for my being on *The Real World*. Perhaps my grandiose goal to be a positive role model and exemplary influence in young people's lives didn't succeed as much as I'd hoped *during* the show, but it may be happening after it.

> I really liked the message that you sent about believing in
> yourself and getting your education. I have done some stupid
> stunts since I have been here at school. It has been my first time
> away from home and I listened to my friends and not to myself.
> I came here determined to get an education, and my dream is to
> be a prosecutor. Listening to you talk tonight has given me a
> new perspective on college. I am going to keep following my
> dreams of a career in criminal law and I am going to listen to
> myself and my family, who I am very close to, and not my
> friends who just want me to party and drink.
>
> —*audience member at lecture*

Someone got the message. . . .

Youth is shattered by misconceptions of "reality." As I talk to more and more young adults by myself now, I become increasingly aware that *The Real World* is a perfect sign of that. Plenty of cast members have had positive past experiences, both professional and educational, that didn't make the cuts. The show seems to accentuate the more social aspects of our lives a bit more than we would have liked. Because we've appeared on international television, you can't deny there *is* an aspect of being a role model. We represent "types" of people in our generation. Although I don't think we're expected to be the leaders of our generation, we are people others can generally relate to. Where we take the exposure is up to us. I would have liked our cast to have come out as leaders, to show the world that business leadership can happen at an early age. We have the youthful energy and the potential talent. If we actually apply ourselves, we can achieve anything.

Obviously, you can see by now that *The Real World* hasn't turned out to be so "real" for me after all. Something goes off inside your head once a camera is pointing at you. It's as if all of a sudden you're an interesting person with a story to tell and there's an obligation to live up to some image, even if it's only in your subconscious. The camera's on you and you're being treated as if your life is something special, when in actuality you just represent a whole bunch of people with similar characteristics who didn't happen to make it to the final cut, for whatever reason. It's a mistake to assume you're anything more than a representation of a larger group of people out there. However, it's important not to lose sight of your individual being and purpose. Unfortunately, it's next to impossible to really be yourself in this sort of environment.

The Present

Sometimes I wonder what would've happened if I had left the show before it ended. Would Nic have chosen me exclusively over other guys? Would I have been faithful to her if we were able to communicate more effectively? I'll never know. Our dilemma wasn't any one person's fault. It was the collective growing pains of two individuals who were lost in emotion and challenged by one another's personal insecurities.

The pain Nic feels from my actions on *The Real World* seem to have hurt her too much to ever commit to me. My suffering comes from wondering if she was ever capable of committing to me in the first place. She's always protecting herself, but in order to truly love, you must take some risks, you recognize and move on from the past hurt, you must believe in the power of the love and look to the future without getting lost in the past. Most importantly, you must first be able to love and forgive yourself. As Thomas Wolfe wrote, "You can run from the disappointments you're trying to forget, but it's only when you embrace your past that you truly move forward."

I can't deny that I totally love Nic and always will, on some level. I've abstained from developing any kind of relationship with other women, including friendships, to allow myself ample time to get to know myself. Facing myself (the good and the bad) and working through it all to develop a new, improved me is a pretty huge breakthrough. As for Nic and me, or Nic alone, we'll just have to wait and see. Don't mess up a relationship if you really love someone.

Dan commented once, "I think the rest of us sunk to this level of little petty squabbling a long time ago, and Joe was always miraculously above it. Within five years, Joe will have written a book about something simply because he wanted to express his love to the rest of the world. It doesn't really matter what it's on; he'll just have written a book. It'll be a beautiful thing."

Our generation is *not* in demise: we're the future of the world. Youthful energy and talent kicks! It's so rewarding to try to make the most of life and not just sit on your butt. There's nothing satisfying about watching the world go by, turning to drugs, alcohol, or sex to escape what's going on in life. Face your life—past, present, and future. Listen to yourself and communicate. Believe in yourself, and others around you will do the same. Generations ahead of us don't have much faith that we'll make something of ourselves or this world. I'd like to prove them wrong!

> I think Joe had a growth experience. At first he took [the show] on as a thing to try. Looking back, I don't think he regrets being part of the show, because he learned so much. I'm very proud of him. I wish him a lot of luck and hope that this book doesn't exploit him any further.
>
> —*my mom (I really love you, Mom.)*

ILLUSTRATIONS

11   Joe and Nic (photographer unknown)

12   Joe, Mike, and Sarah (photo by Patrick J. Farabaugh)

13   Joe with manuscript (photo by T. James)
      Joe in the bike tour (photographer unknown)

14   Joe and Christina (photographer unknown)
      Joe (photographer unknown)

15   Phil and Mary Patane, Christopher, Joe, and Joonmo Ku (photographer unknown)
      Joe and Mike (photo by Sarah)

16   Dan, Arnie, Nic, and Joe (photo by Mike)